Parenting Adventures
through
Paris, Germany and America

This book is not intended as a substitute for the medical advice of physicians. The reader should regularly consult a physician in matters relating to his/her child's health and particularly with respect to any symptoms that may require diagnosis or medical attention. The information is this book is meant to supplement, not replace, the advice of your physician.

This book has suggestions that are helpful pointers on how to raise a child. I am not a doctor and do not claim to be one.

Some names and identifying details have been changed to protect the privacy of individuals.

Copyright © 2017 Marlane Nigbur

All rights reserved.

ISBN-13: 9780998888408
ISBN-10: 0998888400

Parenting Adventures
through
Paris, Germany and America

A Multicultural, Instructive Memoir

MARLANE WINGO

An Open Letter to Soon-To-Be Parents:

Read this book *now*. Read as many books as you can about babies and toddlers. Highlight them in yellow, orange and fuchsia! Go crazy! Whip out those tab markers and post-it notes! Be prepared and devise a plan because when your little darling arrives, there is no time for *I'll just figure it out.*

Your organized, obsessive, fired-up, deviant, misfit author,

Marlane

For my son,
you are Mama's and Papa's
Christmas morning ~ every morning.

CONTENTS

1. Parenting: Learning Another Language   1
The Habits of Visionary Parents

2. Parenting and Sleep   28
Teaching your Child to Sleep

3. Parenting and Food   62
Teaching your Child to Eat

4. Parenting and the Potty   87
Teaching your Child to Go

5. Parenting and the Other   112
Teaching your Child to live in a Multicultural World

    Bonus Chapter 6   158
Passports

    Bonus Chapter 7   177
Cross-border Collaboration

Appendices   202

Chapter 1

Parenting: Learning Another Language
The Habits of Visionary Parents

HELLO MY NAME IS MAMA

"**D**on't have kids," my brother said to me as his three children sprinted through the kitchen. "And if you have one, you'll want more. They're like drugs. You want more and more." Just the usual unsolicited advice from a family member in front of my boyfriend at the time. But I did need the advice. I had never babysat. I had never changed a diaper. At 35 years old, the first diaper I changed was my son Alec's.

Having lived in New York City for ten years during the *Sex and the City* years a whole other world had been hidden from me and the rest of single Manhattan: babies, toddlers and friends with children. If you are single, once a friend has a child you'll never see that person ever again. OK, maybe you'll be invited to a child's first birthday party, but as a singleton it's best to avoid that kiddie "soirée".

The shores of Manhattan act as a massive buffer for singles. A never-never land where one doesn't have to get married. The indulgences outweigh marriage. New York's swagger appealed to me.

My girlfriends were all in the same category. I can't remember one conversation about children over a Sunday brunch the most essential meal for a New Yorker. I never witnessed a mom pushing a stroller in Manhattan, except for Gwyneth Paltrow, and that counted as a celebrity sighting. I blame it on my pre-baby obliviousness. And where would one find a big enough apartment to house this lil' creature and all its *stuff*? Simply, our environment couldn't cater to cribs, mini IKEA circus tents and play kitchen stoves.

More importantly, where would you find a potential partner who worked only forty hours a week in order to have family time? Rest assured, there are very few forty hour a week jobs that can support the exorbitant cost of raising a child in NYC. The logistics and financial responsibility are more than a bit of a stretch for the 99%'er.

Families try their best to stay within New York City, but usually they quickly pack up and move out in their quest for more square footage. Their parental wisdom occurs outside the island's buffers, leaving the rest of us clueless about how to raise a child. There is little insight into this gray area called motherhood.

A LITTLE ADVICE

A few years before having Alec, I made the rookie mistake of asking one of my cousins, Rebecca, stay-at-home-mom of two, "What do you do all day?" I asked it in the most non-judgmental way possible but some questions always come out sounding judgmental. And the reason they seem to sound judgmental is because they usually are.

But my cool as-you-wanna-be cousin, replied back, "I play with my kids. We hang out." This answer was not going to cut it. Especially since I know Rebecca as incredibly independent, successful and a real go-getter. So I did what any naïve person that does not have children would do; I asked again. "No. I mean, what do you *do* all day?" She replied back with the same answer, taking no offense.

I still was not satisfied with her response so, I card-cataloged it in the back of my pea size brain. Until I experienced motherhood, I would never understand her response.

What I expected her to say was, "At the moment, I am teaching them pre-algebra, and I'm currently reading a book on quantitative methods in economics in my spare time."

I was expecting her to say this because I wanted her to say it. A friend of mine told me, "If you go searching for something, you'll find it." When we are not satisfied with an answer, we keep looking and looking until we get the response we want.

I admire my cousin's parenting skills because I like the results: two outstanding, fun boys that should be on *So You Think You Can Dance*. I emailed her asking for a few tips on how she raises her children. "There is not one right way to raise a kid. You just learn what you can and decide what makes sense for you and your hubby." She also made another noteworthy statement about receiving advice from her mother, "While I think my mom did a good job - the best she could do - I do not follow all of her ways. She struggled with that for a long time and still does occasionally. She felt like I was telling her she didn't have a clue, but all I was doing was saying that I am a different person and just because I do it my way doesn't mean I think her way was all wrong."

All the advice from my friends and family, I have implemented in some way into Alec's life. They are a part of me and now embedded into Alec. My teachers that I admire also gave me insight; some are from college, some are from the internet. I watched the YouTube videos "Children Full of Life" about a teacher named Mr. Kanamori from Japan. In a stereotypical country of order and discipline in school, Mr. Kanamori teaches a philosophy of happiness.

"What's the most important thing this year?" Mr. Kanamori.

"To be happy!" students.

"What are we here for?" Mr. Kanamori.

"To be happy!" students.

"We only have one life. So, let's really enjoy it, ok?" Mr. Kanamori.

What a wonderful outlook about life to share with children. He combines academia and life learning. Childhood experiences are of the upmost importance, and he teaches the kids through caring for other people, all the other stuff will fall into place accordingly. But the key thing his students learn is how to solve and work through tribulations as a group because they were taught how to care for other people through many of the teacher's creativity projects, for example, writing in their notebooks. In these notebooks, they express their feelings, compassion, admittance and forgiveness. Mr. Kanamori gives a space for his students to tell their story.

STEREOTYPE LET DOWN

I thought I would finally have my chance to learn all about parenting when we moved to Hamburg, Germany, in the summer of 2012. I imagined journeying to the Mecca of child rearing with nature luvin' parents with a holistic remedy from a scrape to a tummy ache. Parents being "strong-willed Germans" and not buying the Haribo gummy bears eye level to children at the grocery stores. Instead, I found it to be a whimsical world of three-year-old toddlers running around with their *schnullers* (pacifiers) glued in their mouths.

Apparently, it is so incredibly difficult for a German toddler to give up their *schnuller* that Germans call upon the *schnuller* fairy. This fairy is the younger sister of the tooth fairy. The child receives a small present in exchange for their *schnuller*. Great idea until the child wants to return the present back for you know what. Typically, this game lasts for a few months to block out all the crying and tears or what I like to call negotiating. I began to wonder if it is more difficult for the toddler or parents to give up their *schnuller*. It is a great mute button.

One thing is clear, German parents are breeding a whole generation of lawyers. These children have more tactics than an ambulance chasing lawyer. A German child can negotiate and win over their early thirties to late forties parents who have their Ph.D.'s and high-level management skills.

I once witnessed two young boys throwing temper tantrums on the sidewalk. The kind of tantrum where the parent is holding onto one arm trying to get the child to walk while the child's entire body lays lifelessly on the ground. The father said, "Come on! Get up! Ok, what about some cookies? Wouldn't you like some cookies?" One of the boys quickly jumped to his feet and took the bait. The other stayed sprawled out on the ground and said with a cheeky grin, "But I don't want any cookies."

I couldn't believe all the bribery that was going on. Where had the Germans gone wrong? Where were the homemade granola bars? Where were the apples as snacks? Instead of fruit, the children always have a *brötchen* (bread roll) in their hand. In fact, the only time their *schnuller* comes out of their mouth is when a *brötchen* goes in!

Also, I was witnessing zombie parents roaming the streets from sleep deprivation which can be solved with sleep training/learning. But most parents I asked didn't really know about any effective sleep training methods or refuse to use one. Instead they continue on torturing themselves with sleepless nights. Literally, sleep deprivation is a torture technique used by military interrogators. [1]

I was counting on the Germans to help me. I needed to learn everything on how to raise the perfect child. Let me rephrase - a young gentleman. After we found out the sex of the baby, I began telling everyone we were having a boy. My German husband, Jens (pronounced *Yens*), quickly corrected me, "We aren't having a boy. We are having a young gentleman." *Thanks, honey. No pressure.*

All I ever wanted was a happy kid. My parents never let my brothers and I run around the house screaming, jumping on beds and acting like total maniacs. Secretly, I wanted this for my child. I didn't necessarily want screaming but laughter at high soprano decibels were fine with me.

I couldn't accept that the German parents were wimpy and soft-hearted. The stereotype had failed me. I thought I was going to be the one to give in too quickly. And who ever heard of a spineless German? I can assure you there are none unless their first name is Mama or Papa.

Even the German Federal Employment Agency (*Bundesagentur für Arbeit*) website has a quote that was supposed to fulfill my expectations, "Our European neighbors consider the Germans to be well organized, precise and slightly pedantic but also reliable, amiable and sociable." Yes! Yes! Yes! *Ja! Ja! Ja!* I was ready to embrace the *Oberlehrer* (a know-it-all). This is what I needed; however, it turned out to be a pipe dream.

A friend of mine has a T-shirt that blurts out, "Stereotypes are a real time-saver." I would like to apologize now for throwing the labels

American, German, French and Gambian around like we all fit into one bubble-wrapped package.

Chimamanda Adichie gave a superb message about confronting stereotypes in her TED talk, *The danger of a single story*. She states, "...the problem with stereotypes is not that they are untrue but that they are incomplete. They make one story become the only story." [2] Chimamanda describes that by not seeing past our preconceived notions, we can't understand the whole person or country. Also, by not knowing the history or ethnology behind a cultural value can lead to false judgement. All these "stories" are so important because if they are left out, the result is a bunch of - isms: racism, sexism, ageism, heterosexism, classism, ethnocentrism.

AM I CUT OUT TO BE A GERMAN?

Geographically speaking, I thought German child rearing techniques would be fairly similar to France, the U.K., Italy, Spain... ok, I thought everywhere in the European Union. But they couldn't be more different. Borders are there for a reason: to keep things in and to keep things out. And within the EU, they served their purpose. Even with the borders being "open" for twenty years, not enough time has past for much parental exchange. Culture proves once again how powerful it can be against outside forces.

Partly based on my obsession with French movies, I know a little about French culture other than Pepé Le Pew from *Looney Tunes*. I have discovered the only similarities between the Germans and French are that they feed their children an abundance amount of bread, cheese and chocolate – pretty much in that order. And to my surprise, both countries are slim and trim, although Bavarians might have slightly larger waistlines due to all their good beer!

7

Having lived in Orange County, California, I frequented the city of Laguna Beach often and any chance I got – any chance – I went to Jean Paul's Goodies. The best way to describe the owner, Jean Paul, is the Soup Nazi from *Seinfeld*. You better be ready to state your order and have your money ready; not having the exact amount is frowned upon. And no dilly-dallying or as my brother Luke says *lallygagging*. Jean may not greet you with loving arms but his coffee and pastries sure do. This teeny tiny bit of France awaits you in Laguna Beach.

When I told Jean that I was moving to Germany, he fired back, "If you eat German bread...you…you will be as big as that refrigerator!!!" He was pointing to an industrial size refrigerator like a witness pointing to a serial killer across a courtroom. He put me in such frenzy state that my hands were shaking. I left spilling coffee on my arm praying to God that one drop wouldn't hit his floor, and off I went with my usual "small" coffee and croissant. After I devoured every last buttery flake in the front seat of my car, I vowed to eat broccoli and tofu every night until I left for sausage loving Deutschland fearing that I would end up with a refrigerator-shaped body.

Hello carbs! There is a bakery on every corner in Hamburg. Every time I enter a bakery, Jean Paul pops into my head barking in his heavy French accent, "Remember the refrigerator, *mon chérie!*" Americans get such a bad rap from the surplus of fast food joints but what about all the baked goods here?! I agree that in America there is way too much fast food, but there is an obsession like no other when it comes to bread in Germany.

My will power does not last long, and my excuse of pregnancy kicks in. Every morning I ate a croissant or crêpe with two eggs and some cheese I couldn't pronounce. Of course a slice of yummy smoked ham to round out my four-food group meal.

All this amazing food is incredibly accessible. Instead of fast food chains, there are grocery stores offering a superb selection of cheeses, local produce and "real" meat. What makes the grocery stores unique, compared to the States, is that they are user-friendly. They are one-tenth of the size of an American grocery store. You go in and out so easily! In my neighborhood, I can shop at five different supermarkets, a farmers market (twice a week), and even a handful of mom-and-pop specialty food shops. Food is such an important aspect of our lives, but what we consume sets us apart.

I must confess, I have to gripe about one thing regarding the supermarkets. They are closed on Sundays. Every bloody single one of them. One could schedule around this absurdity, but with a baby it is the closest to insanity as a new parent will experience. Most Americans would think it is crazy not to own a car with a baby or child, but somehow we have managed. But I truly don't know how we have managed without grocery stores open on Sundays. And it doesn't stop there. Every store is closed on Sundays; shopping malls, boutiques, pharmacies, any kind of store conceivable. I used to ask my husband when we first moved here how anyone expects to get anything done and how stores expect to make a profit. "There is a time and a place for everything," he would reply. Oh, my German husband.

Please allow me to paint a picture of a typical grocery store scene on a Saturday evening one hour before closing time: Armageddon. Chaos. Pure chaos. Soccer elbows are out. Germans turn into Italians cutting the line.

Ironically, my first German cultural mishap was within two hours of landing in Hamburg; taken place in a grocery store. There was a sales representative giving out free samples of yogurt salad dressing. Me and my little Buddha belly shimmied over for a sample. Of course

9

she speaks English – as does everyone else! I can't tell if Jens is annoyed that I talk to everyone or that I refuse to speak what little German I know.

So the grocery store lady tells me that since I am American, I may not know, but most salad dressings must be consumed within two weeks because like many food items in Germany, it has no preservatives. I tell her where I come from, salad dressings last a year or two in the refrigerator (partially hydrogenated vegetable oils - trans fats - increase shelf life). [3] After she picked her jaw up off the floor, she lectured me on paying attention to expiration dates. I wondered when my expiration date would be for Deutschland.

IT'S DIFFICULT NOT TO COMPARE

At the time we moved, I was three months pregnant. My high-risk OB/GYN doctor in the States rushed the results for the genetic testing. I was fearful I would not have proper health care in Hamburg. I imagined waiting hours to be seen by a doctor and slipping them cash to receive better medical treatment.

But astonishingly, everything was the same as in the U.S. except for the ultrasound equipment. Instead of the 6.0 version, I think they had the 5.0s version. The most shocking part of all my doctor visits was how quickly I was seen by the doctor. It varied from sixty seconds to ten minutes! And it was happening at other offices, too. At the dental office, pediatrician, internist, physical therapist and my general doctor office. Ok, one time I had to wait 25 minutes. I was so peeved because I had grown accustom to not waiting more than six minutes on average. But in my doctor's defense, he prescribed me ten physical therapy treatments and a super-duper, fancy, wrap thing for my excruciating hip pain.

I began to wonder why my OB/GYN doctor was being enormously attentive to me and not rushing through my visit. My appointments always ended with her asking, "Are you sure you don't have any more questions?" Back in the States, I had panic attacks fearing that all my questions wouldn't be answered. I would have a list of questions ready and run through them in lighting speed since I got a total of four minutes with the doctor. Maybe the Germans were trying to get word back to the U.S. that the German health care system is equal if not better than in America. Hmmm…

I slowly began to open up to some of my new German and expat friends how my doctor was showering me with prescriptions. They said this is normal practice. *Really?!* One of my friends said pre and post pregnancy, you can get just about anything you want. She told me about the amazing neck massages she received when pregnant by her physiotherapist.

All my pregnancy tests in the U.S. came out A-ok - relaxing me from finding a doctor immediately in Hamburg. I had put off finding a doctor since I disillusioned myself into thinking Germany was going to be a third world country with Doctors Without Borders.

Also, I faced the challenge of finding an English speaking OB/GYN. But this might have been the easiest part of my entire pregnancy. Since my husband previously lived in Hamburg, I had grandfathered in a few girlfriends through him. One is a nurse, and she recommended an OB/GYN. "Does she speak English?" This seemed to be my only requirement. My friends back in the States would ask me, "Do you like your doctor?" I responded, "Oh, yes, her English is very good." Don't ask me where she studied or how many years of practice. Jeez, where did I think I was living? North Korea? Practically everyone below the age of 65 can speak English in Germany. It was difficult to find someone who didn't speak English until I came upon the German federal agency employees (insert curse word).

Luckily, my only requirement led me to meet some incredibly caring, professional practitioners one of them being my OB/GYN. It's ran by two very patient women who took good care of me throughout my remaining pregnancy. But I did have my doubts after the second visit.

The appointment was going exceptionally well. We were having a friendly conversation; a little chit-chat to ease into the real business.

"How are you getting along in Germany?" asked my doctor.

"Great! I really like it here! There is so much nature even in such a big city. Everything is so green and beautiful," I responded.

"Yes, it is a beautiful time of year. I'm glad you are enjoying it so much," said my doctor.

"Well, there is one thing that really bothers me. All the smokers! I can't believe how many people smoke here! I mean, didn't Germany get the message that smoking is bad for you?!" I exclaimed.

The good doctor frowned and with a lot of attitude, "Well, didn't the United States get the message that eating too much will make you fat?!" she remarked.

Seriously, I almost fell out of my chair from laughing so hard! But I quickly realized that my doctor was not laughing along with me. She was staring me down and tapping her pen on the desk waiting for me to compose myself.

"You know, I smoke occasionally. And it isn't so bad for you," said the DOCTOR.

"Really? You can't be serious. You're a doctor." I tried to make a joke of it to save us from drowning in a deep abyss of uncomfortableness.

"Everything in moderation is ok. I think this is where Americans gets it wrong," stated the German doctor.

Wow! I couldn't believe what I was hearing from a DOCTOR! Unbelievable! What was I going to do? I had found an OB/GYN who I liked and spoke perfect English; however, she thinks smoking is ok in moderation. I did agree with her about eating in moderation but smoking? Come on! I glanced down at my bump that was becoming a rather large bump. I made a baby-belly gut decision and kept going to her.

Later that night, Jens and I discussed the whole smoking phenomenon in Germany. He has definitely seen an increase in smokers. He concluded that Germany's economic rise in the past decade has given Germans more spending power, thus smoking is seen as a form of higher status.

LABOR CLASS WITH A HALF-WIT AND A SMOKING FIEND

I wouldn't mind the smoke so much, but it's everywhere. And the smokers here are so rude about it! They light one up anywhere and everywhere. I can't count how many times I was waiting for a bus or train and someone lights one up right next to me even with my eight month pregnant belly. They don't even try to blow the smoke in the other direction.

A friend in New York City suggests inviting over ex-Mayor Bloomberg to take care of the public smoking problem. If he can ban large soft drinks, he should be able to muzzle these dirty, dog smokers.

After a few months of living in Hamburg, I began to question myself. Maybe I am being too sensitive and should respect the German culture. After all, I am living in their country and should be more understanding with their lifestyle. But yet after another episode with another doctor, I was ready for to protest, boycott and set-up a picket line.

Jens and I signed up for a labor class at our local community center. It was a two-day course held over the weekend led by my *hebamme* (midwife). I was really looking forward to knowing what the heck was going to happen at the birth. One of my uncles had me rolling with laughter when he told me, "It's a lot more fun going in than coming out." Don't we all have an uncle like this?

I could sense Jens' excitement because he finally got to participate in the pregnancy – other than being the donor. He tried to make it to the doctor visits but rarely made it because of work. So, he didn't even mind that the class was taking up an entire weekend.

The weekend came, and we punctually arrived along with the other punctual German couples. As stated in the invitation: coffee, water and cookies will be served. At 9:00am sharp, the *hebamme* announced that everyone was in attendance except one couple. No one minded to start late as it was everyone's first baby, and we all continued to chat with excitement while we waited. But twenty minutes later, the *hebamme* had to begin. Just a few minutes into the class, the last couple leisurely strolled in with their break-the-bank coffees. The *very* soon-to-be mom plopped down with her husband. Later we found out that he is a pediatric surgeon, and she is a lawyer.

At the lunch break, the doctor joined us, but his wife stayed behind. She was tired and wanted to rest at the center. It was a beautiful fall day, and we found a place to eat outside; however, the next table over, someone lit up a cigarette as soon as we sat down. It was a perfect opportunity to complain about smokers to a new lending ear.

The doctor shrugged and said, "Yeah, I don't like it much that my wife smokes."

"You mean…used to smoke," I said.

"No, she still smokes but not as much," said the DOCTOR.

I sat there dumb founded. *Marlane, don't say anything. Just drop it. Drop it right now.* I am positive Jens is thinking the exact same thing. I was correct.

"But you are a doctor. How can you let her smoke?" I questioned. Oops…couldn't hold it in.

"A few cigarettes a day are ok…the placenta can filter most of it out. Also, there are no real proven tests that determine that a few cigarettes a day can have long term effects on the child," said the German doctor.

I was outraged. Blood boiling. Arm pits sweating. Snot bubbles were starting to form like on a wild boar's snout. Here sat across from me, a pediatric surgeon, nonchalantly eating his cheese plate, explaining that smoking is acceptable for pregnant women. I mumbled that pregnancy was difficult and hoped that his wife was able to cope with the stress. Subject dropped…until the next day at lunch.

Back again to our same lunch spot, the wife joined us this time and a few other couples. We had a big group and lunch took some time. We needed to rush back but not before the stupid, ignorant, careless, moron, very pregnant lawyer lady whipped out a cigarette in front of everyone and had a smoke! I glanced at the other pregnant women at the table to get their reaction. No one said a word. No one. Argh! It was all I could do from not ripping that cigarette from her lips and punching her in the face. I thought that it might hurt the baby so, I kept my white-knuckled clenched fist pressed in my lap.

That evening, I emailed a few friends and family back home about what happened. One of my brothers is a nurse in California. He wrote,

"Maybe the guy isn't really a doctor…he just plays one on T.V." My other brother wrote, "She might as well be in Louisiana with a beer in the other hand at a David Allen Coe concert."

I can handle the culture shock, but I refuse to accept the idiocracy. I am taking a stand…a stand against cigarettes and pacifiers. Currently, I am undecided with bread rolls.

WELCOME TO PARIS

Ironically, I observed my first French parenting incident - also involving bread - way back in 2000. I was twenty-four years old and visiting a friend in Paris. I vividly remember walking on a street behind a mom and a young child. Suddenly, they stopped. It was obvious the child was hungry. The mom whipped out a bar of chocolate and broke off a chunk. She stuck it in a piece of baguette and handed it to her child. Voilà! Her version of *la pain chocolat*. They continued walking happily along while I was left knee deep in bewilderment. I couldn't imagine giving a snack like this to a child. In my mind, this was dessert.

How ridiculous of me! Instead of noticing a sweet mother - daughter moment, I only thought about how unhealthy the snack was for the toddler. Many magical things can happen on the streets of Paris if one only removes their judgmental glasses; like watching the eyes of a child light up while receiving a piece of chocolate in a crusty, golden baguette. A short fifteen years later and knowing better, I forgave the Parisian mom.

It is easy to criticize cultural differences and simply not knowing the background information. I find myself too often pointing out the differences instead of recognizing common ground. Being curious about cultural differences is human nature but seeking out the similarities is part of the learning experience, too. The differences are there, but we all want the same for our children. Experiencing cultural exchanges and living in a multicultural society makes for a more harmonious society. And as our world continues to get smaller and smaller; a more peaceful world.

WELCOME TO FRANCE

If Alec speaks three languages (French, German and English), he will have passion like a Frenchman, be strong like a German and seek freedom like an Englishman. Obviously, Alec will first learn German and English. Then French? We are 99.9% sure Alec will go to the International French School (Lycée Antoine de Saint Exupéry) here in Hamburg. He will start the year he turns three. The first couple of years are held in the "l'école maternelle" - France's equivalent to pre-kindergarten. There is structured learning and becoming familiar with the French language, for example, the teacher might explain that today is Tuesday, and Tuesday starts with the letter "T." Everything is age appropriate for developing their motor skills. In addition, Alec will be around native speaking French children and teachers. This is an enormous advantage to learning a language. And, the children at the location in Hamburg will have one hour of German class per day.

And if we ever have to move for Jens' work (he's an aerospace engineer at Airbus), Alec will be able to continue in the French system and have a better transition. There is always a possibility that Jens might be given an opportunity to live in Singapore, Spain, America – you name it. The French education system is exactly the same anywhere in the world so, it makes sense for us. And France is probably the greatest likelihood since the headquarters are located there (Toulouse).

But there are mixed feelings about the French system. Many Germans describe it as too structured and rigorous. From a very young age, children are heavily pressured to get good grades, and there are always talks of their higher education. In my opinion, what's wrong with that? My first reaction is it compares to American ideals. There should always be an outlet where kids can be kids, but at a certain point, students need to be graded on performance.

In Germany, there is plenty of free play at the *kita* (daycare); up until they turn six years old. The first priority is playing outdoors anytime possible. Parents are not encouraged to teach their children to read or write. Learning how to read begins in the first school grade. Most German parents and teachers agree that children will be bored in class if they already know how to read. [4]

By the time Alec is two and a half years old, he knows the ABC song, can name roughly fifty percent of the letters and the sounds. And I'm now starting to work on "blending." For example, "Alec, come s-i-t down." When speaking to Alec, I will take one simple word and individually sound out each letter then say the word. And it's working. Repetition! Repetition!! Repetition!!!

I told a German girlfriend of mine that Alec knows the ABC song, and when I point to letters, he can name most of them. "What?! My daughter is four years old and can't even write her name!"

One day I'm at the gym getting dressed, and next to my locker I hear a water bottle drop and a very American *uh, oh* followed. Her mom is French and her dad is American, and she grew up in Germany. She actually attended Lycée in Hamburg. It's the same school we want to send Alec.

When it was time for her and her husband to decide on schools for their two daughters, they also thought about Lycée. They went for an interview and a tour of the school. They were a bit horrified at all the well-behaved children. She said in the kindergarten classrooms, the children sat in their own little chairs and desks. And on the playground, they witnessed a teacher giving instructions on how to ride a bike. The children had to stay in the bike lane and ride behind each other in a straight, single line. Sorry if I come across like a nun who whips kids knuckles with a wood ruler, but the French school system impressed me.

Overall, the woman did not have many positive things to say; however, towards the end of our conversation, she worked herself up to say, "Probably if I wasn't working, I would send my girls there." She explained that the hours at Lycée did not work with her part-time job. I told her as of fall 2015, the school was offering hours up until 6pm. This made her pause. But she quickly followed it up with, "Well, the traffic is really horrible around that area."

"You could move closer to the school. That's what we are doing so, we can walk or ride our bikes there," I said.

"You are moving so your child can be closer to the school?" said the mom.

Oh, god. Boy, did I get a look from her.

"But you live in such a nice neighborhood! Why would you move your whole life there?" she questioned.

She was correct. We lived in a beautiful area called Hoheluft-West in the Eimsbüttel borough. Our apartment was built in the early nineteen hundreds and has hard-wood floors, tall ceilings, moldings and two small balconies. The kind of European apartment I dreamed about. Jens and I agreed that we wanted to live in an urban area where we could have easy access to cafés and restaurants.

"It's only a fifteen minute car ride away and Lokstedt isn't so bad. It has its perks like the zoo and the forest," me. Coincidentally, I didn't mention that I don't support zoos. But the forest has some wild life, and it's thick with towering green trees. And there's a lush park nearby with a pond, ducks and geese.

"Why don't you just drive him there?" she said not backing down.

"Like you said, traffic. We'll have a six minute walk to school through a park. Also, we want Alec to be close to his school friends and have his own little community there," I answered nervously, waiting for her to pounce on me again.

I wanted to follow it up with, "Plus, our commitment to our son's education is very important to us." But miraculously, I was able to keep my mouth shut.

At this point, the half French woman thought I was out of my mind. I could see that the guilt from not sending her daughters to the school had vanished. I suppose we both got something out of the conversation.

ON BECOMING BILINGUAL

From my global, expat, chameleon-like friends, I found the best way for a child to learn more than one language is for each parent to speak one language (one parent one language - OPOL). No mixing! This is important to "foster balanced bilingualism." [5] Since Alec was born, I have only spoken English to him. Jens only speaks German to Alec. Furthermore, Jens and I speak English to each other. The major advantage with OPOL is that the child will have a mother and father tongue - a native speaker in both languages.

"Most researchers believe that the language of the community (e.g. the language of the country) is the dominant language of bilingual speakers." [6]

Even my mother-in-law approved of our teaching ways! We received a packet of information via the post mail from her saying we were doing it the right way. Wow! Also, our HNO *Hals-Nasen-Ohren* (neck-nose-ears) doctor affirmed that our teaching style of OPOL is the most effective.

French will sort of fit in with the same concept since it will most likely only be spoken at the French Lycée daycare/school. The bottom line is there needs to be clear boundaries. When Alec learns and speaks French, it will be with a physical/geographical boundary.

I talk a lot to Alec. I am a jabber mouth. I can run my mouth all day long and then some. A natural. And parents talking non-stop is probably the best way for children to learn a language. But I do have to control myself and give him an opportunity to speak. I try not talk over him when I notice he is trying to formulate how to say something. In the beginning, I asked a lot of yes and no questions. Then I would slowly work my way into open ended questions.

I think it would have helped if I taught Alec more sign language. Not a lot but a few simple signs. I don't know why I didn't teach him more words. I did teach him "all done" in sign language for when he is finished with his meal. And on his own, he found more uses for it. For example, when I have finished reading him a book or when he has gotten out every single last toy truck from his basket and gives the sign for "all done."

Another tip that I learned a little too late is to speak where your child can see your mouth. I found this out at Alec's *kita* (daycare). There was one little girl in particular that was by far the most advanced in her speech (German). I was overly observant with them because the girl's vocabulary and speech was incredible for her age.

She should have been on some child's talent show. I began to notice what her mom did differently. The mother always made sure her daughter saw her face when she spoke. The mom would bend down to be eye level, and her daughter would watch the mom's mouth intently. There is definitely something to this method. One day I mentioned to the mom that she should start teaching her daughter English. I think she took it as a joke rather than a compliment or idea.

A valuable tip I received from a mom raising a bilingual child is that when Alec mispronounces something wrong like *tar* instead of *car*, don't point out the mistake by saying, "No. That's not correct. You are supposed to say car." Parents should just repeat back the correct way to say the word or phrase with emphasis on the word.

BILINGUAL PROGRESS

Alec is now sixteen months and mostly speaks German except for an English *no*. But he can say - almost flawlessly - some random words like horse and orange juice in English. Alec understands everything I say, and I know he can speak English but chooses not to. I'm guessing it's because he started German *kita* at twelve months old. The daycare staff and children only speak German there. Parents raising bilingual to multilingual children tell me to be patient, continue and repeat.

At the moment, he says *bitte* (please) a lot. I feel disappointed since I am constantly trying to teach him please and thank you in English, but grateful he does understand the concept of please. And if *bitte* is one of his first words, then I am extremely content that he is learning polite behavior.

Reporting back at seventeen months, I am thrilled with Alec's language progress. And his main caregiver at his *kita* says his vocabulary level is appropriate for his age; especially since he is being raised bilingual. But a turning point happened with the whole bilingual thing. The other day I had a picture book and asked Alec to point to the tree. He pointed to the tree and said *baum* (tree). He understood the word in English and spoke back in German. He made the connection!

Is it just me or do girls start talking earlier than boys? I noticed at Alec's *kita* girls were naming colors left and right. This was when Alec was around eighteen months. I immediately began teaching him, and after one month, he picked it up. There have been countless examples where I feel like I am talking to a wall. And then, poof! He finally gets it.

At nineteen months, he still isn't saying please or thank you in English which is unnerving. Instead, his favorite word these days is *mehr* (more). He will tell me when he needs help. It sounds more like the word *up*, but he's saying it in the right context. At twenty-one months, Alec speaks 75% German and 25% English. Rarely he mixes them together, too. I correct him by saying, "Mama says car. Papa says auto."

By two years, Alec has found his style of learning new vocabulary. I teach him a new word, and he uses it for a few days. Then he wants to know the translation in German by asking, "Papa says?" Once he masters how to pronounce it in German, Alec drops the English word, and I hardly hear it again. I constantly have to repeat it in English while he happily uses the German word over and over.

But Alec did give me the most glimmering, radiant gift a parent can receive in the early years: the first time he said *I love you*. In English!

I had just disciplined Alec and sent him to his corner. "The corner" works for us, but sometimes Alec does make a little game out of it.

After he sits there for about sixty seconds supposedly thinking about what he did wrong, I come over and say to him, "Can you tell mama your sorry?" He says while nodding his head, "I'm sorry." Then I ask him, "Do you know what I'm sorry means? It means you won't do it again." I learned this parenting tip from my friend Whitney about the meaning of *I'm sorry*.

Then I follow it up with a big hug, and I say, "I love you." This is when I heard, "I uv ew." I melted like butter on a hot pan. The second time I heard it was when Jens and Alec were leaving to go for a walk. As I was closing the front door, I called out, "Have fun! I love you!" I heard a howl from the stairwell, "I uv ew!"

With a grocery list of positives outweighing the negatives, a few of my friends and family can't understand why we want Alec to start learning three languages at such an early age. Because the sooner the better! Children are more likely to learn more languages between one and four years. [7] And they are worried that Alec will be confused and not even learn English correctly. Dr. Fred Genesee's study found that "though there are no studies on trilingual children, bilingual children acquire two languages as naturally as one, and at the same rate - without confusion." [8]

When heading into parenthood, one hears many stories of children with disabilities. My thoughts go out to those families. Even the most minor disability is heart wrenching. But when one has a healthy child, why hold them back from their full potential? We don't give babies and toddlers enough credit. They are capable of doing so many things if only given the chance. And later in the book, I will discuss that even with Alec's limited hearing, he became fluent in English, German and French by three and a half years old. Chapter 5 goes into more detail on how to learn more than one language, but the secret it to start before the age of three.

"McLaughlin (1978), for example, proposed that after the age of 3, languages are no longer learnt in the same manner as first languages, and others have since argued that after three a variety of linguistic developments are limited by neurological change in the brain. Long (1990), Hyltenstam and Abrahamsson (2003), Obler et al. (1982) and Hahne and Friederici (2001), for example, have all argued that learners exposed to a second language after the age of 3 represent this language differently in the brain from their mother tongue." [8]

THE FRENCH WOMAN

While my son is destined and heavily pressured to learn three languages or more, I have struggled with my second. I embrace my mother tongue and enjoy meeting up with my English speaking friends. For example, a friend invited me to an English play performed by the Hamburg Players club. I discovered for a small membership fee, one could join in their group activities, for example, play readings and improvisation sessions. I never wanted to be an actress, but my interest in the theatre is strong. And more importantly, they only speak English. Delightful!

Looking for a bit of adventure and continuing to brush up on my English skills, I planned to meet a girlfriend and attend a Girl Gone International party. It's just as you would imagine. The group usually has a different theme, and that particular evening was to wear a fun hairpiece. I dug out an unworn headband with a black rose that I bought five years ago at Forever 21 for a dollar. Now I finally had proof to show Jens how important it is not to get rid of anything.

I arrived late, but my friend was nowhere in sight. I happily sat at the bar and gulped down a glass of repugnant red wine. It didn't help my frozen feet. I rode my bicycle over in heels. It was the middle of winter but how many times do I get a chance to dress up and wear something other than orthopedic, easy slip-on, walking shoes?

I would like to note that wearing sweatpants outside the house in Hamburg is an inconceivable idea. In three years, I can count on one hand how many times I have seen people wearing sweatpants outside their homes. I should have chased them down and introduced myself since they were most likely North American.

Wearing any kind of stretchy, work-out or yoga pants other than to the gym is also a no-go. I have no idea how many times I have heard, "Oh, are you making sport today?" The German way of asking if you are working out or going to the gym. But I was only dropping off Alec at *kita* (daycare). Don't they know that half my wardrobe consists of black, stretchy, work-out pants? I could open a store called 'Black Stretchy Pants for Every Occasion' and make a fortune. (Oh, lululemon has already beat me to it.) A moms' armor are black, stretchy pants. They fit our fluctuating body weight, hide baby/toddler handprints, easy to wash with no ironing, comfortable for hours of Lego playing on the floor, easy to chase a kid that has transformed into a bottle rocket shooting through the grocery store isles. Also, great for when you are too tired to change into your pajama pants and can go straight to bed. Jens finds this utterly disgusting. I'm aware it's not hygienic, but let's get real; it happens.

Returning to the bar story, I began chatting with a woman from Spain and another from Iran. My friend soon came and introduced me to some other witty, interesting women. But the real treat was about to come. I met the most quintessential French woman. She had cutout a bird from a magazine and bobby-pinned it to her hair. It would have looked like a dinner plate on my head, yet she looked like a mannequin in a Bergdorf Goodman window display.

She completely dominated the conversation amongst the three of us with a bunch of *lah lah lah's*. She had replaced her conductor's baton with a cigarette. The French tend to glamorize thin women puffing away. But she was magnificent. She definitely didn't own any black, stretchy, work-out pants. To keep her talking, I would ask a question when she took a drag of her cancer stick, and she chimed back in with another monologue.

"How long have you lived in Germany?" me.

"A few years," says the French mother.

"Oh, I bet your German is really good," me.

"God, no. German is so...lah, lah, lah. I have no time to learn German. When I come home from work, I want to relax and enjoy life with my family. We cook together and play and lah lah lah. And when the children go to bed, I want to have sex with my husband. Who has time for German!?" she proclaims.

As she took another drag, I tried my darndest to think of another question that could come after the "sex with my husband" comment, but I had nothing. Only the word *bitch* came to mind.

Later that evening, my friend and I analyzed her to death: a working mom with two children and wants to have sex with her husband every night. So, this is what the rest of the world is up against: The French Woman.

Chapter 2

**Parenting and Sleep
Teaching your Child to Sleep**

WHY SLEEP TRAINING

In the first draft of this book, I had the following paragraph at the end of the chapter. But because of its importance, I moved it to the beginning.

When it comes to sleep training, both parents need to support each other and know the benefits. If a parent is having a hard time grasping the concept and against sleep training, explain the outcome when one doesn't implement any sleep *education* - all the gruesome, nightmare stories of sleepless, cranky babies that continues into childhood and into the parent's bed for *years*.

"Infants, pre-toddlers, and toddlers who suffer from the lack of healthy naps and continuous nighttime sleep may experience chronic fatigue. Fatigue is a primary cause of fussiness, daytime irritability, crankiness, discontentment, colic-like symptoms, hypertension, poor focusing skills, and poor eating habits". [1]

As soon as I found out I was pregnant, I reached out to my family and friends with children – mostly living in Texas and California - for book recommendations. Before moving to Hamburg, I stocked up on 'how to' baby books in English. I imagined being stranded on some remote island where I wouldn't have access to Amazon. I read and re-read every book, and then read a third time to highlight and Post-it.

Not having my own mother in the same hemisphere didn't help my paranoia. And I bought a ton of folic acid and multivitamins in case I wound up on that deserted island again. By the way, do not take your vitamins and/or iron supplements with tea or coffee. They can reduce the absorption by fifty percent! [2]

In addition to the books that my friends and family suggested, I received some great parenting advice. But I would like to point out one tip that was always mentioned with great intensity: sleep training. After googling sleep training and realizing it was not a baby and mommy class, I had an eureka moment. I would definitely implement this strategy. Never could I imagine how beneficial this is for a baby and the parents' sanity. Never.

After hearing countless, awful, unthinkable, alarming, mind-blowing, horrendous, depressing stories from parents about their baby, toddler, or even a five-year old's sleep problems, prompted me to write this book.

Here are a few more that will make you cringe: 2 year old bedtime of 11pm, 1 ½ year old relentlessly standing and crying in crib every night until parents take him into their bed (this continued until he was three), 7 month old waking every forty-five minutes during the night, sleeping in the parent's bed at 4 years old, and the many toddlers still not sleeping through the night.

When Alec was a baby, parents would ask if Alec had started to sleep through the night. I responded with a gentle apologetic *yes*. They usually add, "Oh, you got so lucky." No, luck had absolutely nothing to do with it. I owe it all to sleep training methods. I also would like to tell them he started sleeping through the night at nine weeks old. But in this case, it would not be bragging rights. For sleep-deprived parents, it would be an excruciating, hurtful comment.

I did want to help. I wanted to share my know-how and tell them all the benefits of sleep training. But after numerous awkward conversations of trying to explain, I gave up. This was the usual conversation:

"What?! Alec started sleeping through the night at nine weeks old?" ~ a German mom

"Yes, and by three months, he was sleeping ten hours." ~ me

"Really?! Wow, what a good baby! That's incredible." ~ a mom

"Well, we did sleep training." ~ me

"What's sleep training?" ~ a mom

"It's when you have your baby on a set feeding and sleeping schedule. And then around two months, you have to let your baby cry themselves to sleep for the first two or three nights." ~ me

"Oh, god. I could never do that!" ~ a mom

"No, wait. Really. It's just a few nights. It took Alec only two nights." ~ me

"Oh, no. I could *never* let my baby cry. Not even for a second." ~ a mom

By this point, the conversation turns awfully uncomfortable, and the parent (mom) is shaking their head looking for the nearest exit. One mother-in-law remarked to my friend, "We don't let our babies cry in Germany." Oh, really? Good luck with that one, lady.

And it's not only the baby that suffers from sleepless nights; the whole family endures this misery. The severity of not having some sort of sleep program is unmeasurable. Actually, it is measurable. The of crying it out method for two or three nights is far worse than three years of suffering. Let's do the math:

365 nights x 3 years = 1,095 nights

So, we have 2 or 3 nights of crying it out versus 1,095 sleep deprived nights. Numbers don't lie. Which would you prefer?

I even stumbled upon the *Baby Whisperer* honing in on this three-day concept. This magical consecutive three days (or less) works wonders in fading out old behaviors and establishing correct ones. [3]

In all honesty, I have only met one German parent in Hamburg whose baby slept through the night starting at seven months old. And that particular baby was the second child. Most babies start sleeping through the night at one year of age but have difficulty falling to sleep at nighttime and trouble with naps for the next few years. The parents better have room for three!

And naps are just as important. Babies and toddlers need to re-fuel in order to make it through the day. One mom says her 18-month-old son will not take naps at home, only at daycare.

"What happens on the weekends when he doesn't have a nap? What time does he go to bed?" I asked.

"Usually around 5:30pm," said the mom.

"And when does he wake-up?" I questioned.

"Around 5am," she replied.

"Ouch!" I exclaimed.

"But sometimes he is so tired, he will not fall asleep until really late," remarked the mom.

When a child is sleep deprived, they can work themselves up to fight sleep. When fatigue sets in, it's hard to fall asleep. It will always be a struggle at nighttime. The combination of a good night's rest and an appropriate amount of nap-time will make the difference in a good or bad day. It first starts with the baby's/toddler's mealtime. If a baby is tired and cranky, then they will not eat. They will cry and scream until a parent offers something they can't refuse. And if a baby/toddler eats applesauce and cookies for lunch, then the result will be a cranky baby again in an hour.

BEGINNINGS OF SLEEP TRAINING

About one-third of American babies sleep through the night at 11 weeks. [4] And as Pamela Druckerman, an American author living in Paris, found out babies sleep through the night "usually after two or three months" in France. [5] Wish to achieve this? Here we go!

With Alec, we wanted to begin his sleep training at eight weeks old, but he had a cold. So, a week later we began. At nine weeks old, he slept eight to nine hours straight - no nursing, no diaper change. By the tenth and eleventh week, nine to ten hours. Then at three months, he was sleeping through the night for ten to twelve hours. He reached his "peak" just at four months old sleeping twelve hours.

But some sort of training did start from his birth. During the day, we tried to keep Alec in the light. No closed curtains; not even when taking naps. Please do not place your newborn directly under a window with sunlight beaming in. The idea is for the baby to understand day and night, and they can do this! We have a hormone called melatonin that signals to our body when it is daytime and nighttime. [6]

And even in the first month, when the baby starts to cry during the night, wait a moment before picking them up. By consoling them so quickly, it could start a pattern of them waking often in the night. [7]

The French are known to do this, too. The method is used on newborns to wait to see if the baby can soothe itself - waiting a few minutes before rushing to pick up a crying baby. [8] In all honesty, the first few weeks of Alek's life if he even made a peep, I was hovering over him checking his breathe and making sure he was still alive. And if he was crying, I picked him up immediately.

Don't think they are capable of learning so young? When a newborn, baby or toddler learns, they do not learn in one instance; gradually they learn with repetition. In two months, the baby will know the difference along with more guidance.

Also at birth, my mother told me to breastfeed Alec for long periods; no more than thirty minutes in total. Don't let a newborn nurse for just a few minutes on and off. And she reiterated not to eat spicy foods or acidic foods like tomatoes and orange juice which could upset Alec's tummy. "Caffeine and alcohol also enter the breast milk, and limiting their use is recommended while breastfeeding". [9] And try not to eat/drink too much dairy and gas-inducing foods like broccoli and beans at one meal. [10]

I was very fortunate to have Alec nursing on my breast immediately after the birth. He hopped on me a couple of times like a little frog, and the nurse helped him latch onto my breast. I was flooded with emotion.

A big safety issue to avoid with a newborn is to never let them sleep in the parents' bed. We had a crib - with one side open - pushed up against to my side of the bed. The crib mattress was level to our mattress. That way for the first couple of months we were able to be with Alec, but he was not directly in our bed.

I received an excellent tip from a pediatric osteopath at the hospital; let your newborn suck mom's pinky finger for soothing. It doesn't work that great with dad's big fingers. So, note for soon-to-be-moms, trim your fingernails before going to hospital for labor! The pinky trick also works great as to not get your baby in the habit of falling asleep while nursing. At about two weeks old, I tried my best to keep Alec awake after nursing. *It's difficult - I ain't gonna lie.* I read in a ton of places that moms shouldn't nurse their baby to sleep, and my mother concurred. Try your hardest to put your baby down before they fall asleep. [11] This is one of the beginning steps of sleep training. It teaches the baby to go back to sleep without feeding/milk or rocking or singing or driving around in a car for two hours because nothing else seems to work.

Of course I nursed Alec during the night the first two months. A baby's stomach is not big enough to store all their milk they need to get through the night. But when Alec was crying during the night - not from hunger - I gave him my pinky. I would lay in my bed and stretch my arm out into his open crib and have him suck on my finger. He would fall asleep happily - mama, too!

Jens and I were in complete agreement about not giving Alec a pacifier, only my finger as his pacifier and the rare occasions of a pacifier, for example, in a restaurant. It worked great! The first three months babies like to comfort suck and pacifiers and substitutes are useful, but after this time, take them away as to not make a bad habit. [12]

In Germany when Alec was under two years old, parents would ask me, "Does Alec take a pacifier?" I got this question a lot since it is more common for a baby/toddler to be seen sucking on a pacifier than without one. My response was a quiet humble *no*, but secretly inside, I was beaming rainbows that could make a Leprechaun drunk.

HOW TO GET YOUR BABY TO SLEEP THROUGH THE NIGHT

In order for a eight week old baby to sleep through the night, it entails them getting enough milk during the day. At eight weeks, I had Alec on a 2 ½ to 3 hour eating (nursing) schedule. Regarding breast feedings and tracking my baby's growth, I followed the website *Baby Center*, and the advice of Alec's pediatrician. In addition, I heavily depended on the book *On Becoming Baby Wise: Giving Your Infant the Gift of Nighttime Sleep* by adviser Gary Ezzo and pediatrician Robert Bucknam. Another great book is by Simone Cave and Dr. Caroline Fertleman, *Your Baby Week by Week*.

The schedule is an easy concept at eight weeks: nurse (thirty minutes), then play (one hour), then sleep for 1 to 1 ½ hours. Write or type out the schedule, keep it updated and post for viewing. The times obviously change as the night time sleep increases. The schedule will vary depending on your baby's wake and bed time. In the beginning, try to aim for a bed time of 10:00pm. I gave two different wake time examples at eight weeks. Check-out the second part of this chapter for Alec's sleep/eat schedule from birth to four years.

I kept our updated schedule at the entry table so, Jens always had easy access to it. I found that emailing a copy is not enough but whatever works for your family. This schedule should rule the house. Also, if there are more children, it's ideal for them to see the schedule and be familiar with the routine. Either way, it's smart to have a physical sheet of paper displayed somewhere of importance.

Keeping a schedule is not a ground breaking concept. There are many interpretations, for example, Tracy Hogg of *Secrets of the Baby Whisperer* recommends a schedule called E.A.S.Y. (Eating, Activity,

Sleeping, You). It's an insightful book, and I found most of the information agreeable; however, I wasn't comfortable with all the suggestions.

Most often at eight weeks, if your baby is following scheduled feedings and naps, they will start sleeping seven to eight hours continuously during the night. [13]

At eight weeks, if your baby is waking many times during the night and refuses to fall asleep on his own, it is time for some version of crying it out (C.I.O.); the horrible, dreaded phrase. But let me preface by saying that it's only for three nights. And it's not more than an hour, and parents can check-in on their baby. Even Jo Frost (*Supernanny*) uses almost the exact same technique, but it's called *controlled-crying* starting at the age of six months. [14]

I know how difficult it is to let your child cry for even one minute. I bawled outside Alec's door when it was time for C.I.O. I vividly remember thinking about one of Sheryl Crow's songs, "No one said it would be easy, but no one said it'd be this hard." But when Alec turned nine weeks, I was tired. Jens was tired. We were arguing because the exhaustion was beyond belief. We were ready.

I put Alec in his crib. A kiss from mama and papa, and we left his room. We cracked the door and waited in the hallway. I stayed strong by squeezing Jens' hand. In my other hand, I clenched my cell phone watching the clock.

The first night was about forty-five minutes of crying and the second night for thirty minutes. Luckily, our third night was only a couple of minutes. And it was over! Done! That was it! Here's what we did for the first couple of nights:

After eight minutes of crying, go into your baby's room but only for a very short time; maybe ten to fifteen seconds and leave. Try not to pick up your baby; rather just a gentle touch and letting your baby hear your voice. [15] If you do pick up the baby, hold the child for a moment. [16] Then after ten minutes, go back in and repeat. Again, only go in for ten to fifteen seconds. Try the next time at twelve minutes. I know it is painful, but please remember you are giving your baby a priceless gift - the ability to sleep. Repeat these intervals. On average, it can last thirty-five minutes. [17] Alec took forty-five minutes the first night. Start again the following evening. Don't let all that crying from the night before go to waste or you will have to go through it all over again at some point. The second night is much shorter; sometimes only 15 minutes. [18] Remember it will only take a few days but being consistent is key!

In France, most babies are sleeping through the night but not always. When this occurs, "French experts usually recommend some version of crying it out" if it doesn't happen by four months. [19]

When parents are ready for the two or three nights of C.I.O., make sure your baby is completely healthy. That also means no runny noses. It is an uncomfortable enough experience to go through. On that note, anytime a baby/toddler has a runny nose, put a towel underneath the mattress on one side - where the baby's head rests. The mattress should only be tilted up about three inches. It will help drain the mucus so, the baby can breathe easier. It doesn't work 100% but any little bit helps. Our *hebamme* (midwife) gave us this tip.

BEDTIME ROUTINE

To help the baby learn the concept of sleeping through the night around two months is with a bedtime routine. A few repeated steps go a long way, but the steps must be exact every time. [20] Read a book to your baby, your choice. Babies love to hear their parents' voices.

Pick out whatever book you fancy because they won't know the difference yet. Read a newspaper, recipes, diary, comic strip, dictionary, whatever! Anything for them to hear your voice. As your child gets older, they will love books. As a toddler, it's Alec's favorite activity besides a visit to the playground.

For the first two months of Alec's life, I read ten minutes of a novel to Alec in the evenings. A German girlfriend gave me a children's book, *The Brothers Lionheart* by Astrid Lindgren as a baby gift. The Swedish book is rather violent for a children's book since it has a reoccurring theme of death. I would have never selected this book had I known.

Turns out, a lot of German fairy tales are scary and creepy, too, for example, *Der Struwwelpeter* (Shockheaded Peter) by Heinrich Hoffmann. I haven't taken the time to translate the book word for word, but the illustrations are of a boy getting his thumb cut off, a girl on fire, a child starving to death, a boy drowning…you get the idea. I also didn't realize how many modern day fairy tales and movies are inspired (perhaps stolen?) from the Brothers Grimm (German) and Hans Christian Andersen (Danish).

Next is a diaper change, followed by a specific lullaby. I stress specific because anytime you put your baby down for naps or bedtime they need to hear this song as a clue that it is time to sleep. But here's a warning parents, pick one that you like because you will sing it for about two years. No joke. When Alec was about one and a half, I stopped singing his lullaby at nap time but continued with it at bedtime. Learn from my mistake. I chose a song without thinking the impact it would have, and I barely knew the words. Truthfully, I still don't. I made up the last half of the song *Hush, Little Baby*. When Alec hears those lyrics, his eyelids go heavy, he rubs his eyes with his small fists, and is ready to lay his head down.

Instead of a favorite "blankie" for newborns/babies, our *hebamme* (midwife) recommends a very thin silk scarf. If the scarf ends up on the baby's face while sleeping, he or she should still be able to breath. Alec's scarf was about twelve by twelve inches. Be sure to buy at least two scarves since it will get a lot of use. A soft, snuggly object to signal to your little one that it's time to sleep. Until Alec was one and a half years old, he slept with his scarf. It also made an easier transition at *kita* when he began since this is where he takes his daily nap. Around one year of age, Alec began bringing his favorite teddy bear to bed as well and to the dinner table. Bears get hungry, too!

I highly recommend using an infant sleep sack, too. I prefer the ones with arm openings. I bought one for the spring/summer and another for the fall/winter months. One of Alec's babysitters is from Brazil, and she had never seen or heard of a sleep sack until living in Germany. They are also widely known in America and France. No one should ever put a blanket or any object in a crib that could suffocate a newborn/baby; not even a stuffed animal or pillow. [21]

Jens went back to work when Alec was three weeks old. This is the time when we moved Alec into his own room. We also put a twin size bed for me to sleep in. Again, we pushed his crib up to my bed with one side open. I figured one of us should at least get a good nights sleep. Since Jens had to work, it should be him.

I was able to catch up on my sleep when Alec took his naps during the day. Until Alec was three months old, I slept in his room every night. But after three months, I have slept in mama's and papa's bed. When Alec woke up in the morning, we always brought him to our bed for his first breastfeeding of the day and lots of snuggles. These were our Christmas mornings. Now Alec is four years old. Seeing our precious sleepy head shuffle down the hall to breakfast and giving him his first hug for the day is still our favorite moment.

CHALLENGES AND JUDGEMENTS

The hardest part with sleep training is sticking to the schedule, but the pay off is tremendous. I can't imagine what my friends have gone through, excuse me, *still* going through. Parents waking up every two hours with one to two-years-olds. Moms still having to sleep in their three-year-olds room. Six-year-olds only going to sleep with mom or dad sitting on the edge of the bed. One year olds only taking one nap a day, sometimes none. This makes for a hellish day, and it's incredibly difficult to put them to bed at night. When it's 7:30pm, Alec's head touches the mattress and in a few minutes he is fast asleep until 6:30am.

And because Alec is such a good sleeper, I was able to write this book. Since I am able to get a good night's sleep, I wake up feeling well rested and have energy to work. Some young mothers I knew would drop their child off at daycare, and then go home to take a nap before beginning their day (again).

Over the past few of years, I have spoken to many German parents casually about sleep training. The resistance I receive is when the baby has to C.I.O. for two or three nights. I explain over and over that it usually only takes two nights. I explain about the endless benefits, but the parents can't seem to think past words 'crying it out'. As soon as a I say this phrase, their head shakes no and a hand goes up to signal *stop talking*.

I would give the German-moms living in my apartment building updates about Alec's sleep progress. Honestly, I don't think they believed me. All my German-mom friends were skeptical, and sometimes I got the feeling that they thought I was being a bit deceptive.

While my mother does not approve of the C.I.O. method, she did agree with some sort of schedule. She said at around three to four months of age babies should only be fed every three to four hours.

Of course I asked her many things about my infancy. She admitted that she didn't remember much about me but instead my oldest brother. But she did tell me to check my baby book for my dates of growth, accomplishments and habits.

I dug it out and found that she actually had recorded a lot of information about me. It prompted me to ask my oldest brother for his baby book thinking it would be a gold mine of information on how to raise a baby/child. He has misplaced it. Argh!

Also in my baby book, I discovered a one page, pink pamphlet titled *Care of Your Infant* given from the doctor in 1976. This one page, tri-folded piece of paper would have come in so handy!

And there it was in print: A SCHEDULE. "Feed every 3 to 4 hours when hungry. If baby wants to eat sooner than 3 hours, try to stall him by giving him water or a pacifier." [22] More research over the past forty years has shown that parents are not suppose to introduce water to a healthy baby until six months of age but having a schedule still stands strong.

I am not joking. I wish someone would have given me this pamphlet at the time when Alec was born. In the hospital, I had a short consultation on breastfeeding, and they showed Jens different positions of how to hold a baby. That was it - *good luck*. Although, I am extremely grateful that Alec and my body cooperated so well with breastfeeding.

I pored over the pink leaflet looking for anything regarding sleep.

Nothing. But I did find this statement under the paragraph titled *Babies are Babies*, "Even a well baby will probably cry for a little with each day and could cry for an hour or so occasionally without doing himself any harm." What?! Wow! I found this to be so fascinating that this was acceptable in the seventies.

Sure we had problems every once in a while when it was time for Alec to sleep. We learned one smart solution with using white noise. Parents can soothe their baby to sleep by a white noise or sound machine. Buy one! A loud one! Because of the loudness, we were able to go easily in and out of his room to check on him without worrying about the squeaky wood floors. Usually, ten minutes was enough, and he was out. We started with a hairdryer, and Alec got use to the noise. It worked wonders! But definitely a safety issue. Please don't follow my lead on the hairdryer. In hindsight, we should have bought a proper noise machine but had no idea it would work so well.

Very rarely did we have a problem with putting Alec to bed. But from six months to a year, this seemed to be a time when he had a few problems falling to sleep at bedtime. About once or twice a week, we had to use the white noise trick. Don't forget it when traveling. It will save you!

Many parents wait till six months to start sleep training. I am not sure why this is a popular age to begin. Just because it is half way through the first year and a nice round number doesn't mean it's the proper time. It could possibly be one of the worst times. There are many physical and mental developments at this point. [23] Any time there are changes happening with your little one, don't add extra stress and pressure with something new. Parents run into three major problems around this age:

- The first is teething. Not a good idea to introduce a new routine.
- Also, babies will usually have a growth spurt at six months.
- Lastly, at six months, this is the point when babies start eating solids. [24]

My *hebamme* was strongly against our sleep training methods. She made it very clear that she didn't approve of a baby C.I.O. until they are at least six months old. And she followed it up with, "Even at six months, it's still too soon." Also, she believed in the philosophy, *never wake a sleeping baby*. With sticking to a schedule, parents are going to have to wake up the baby to follow the routine. [25] Again, this is to ensure the baby gets enough milk during the day as to not wake-up in the middle of the night hungry. Also, if the baby sleeps too long during the day, he or she will be awake for longer periods during the night. And no one wants that.

But I cherished my midwife's wisdom for everything else. She was incredibly helpful and loving to me and Alec. With my mother being on the other side of the world, my midwife was there for us.

THE ROUTINE: BIRTH TO FOUR YEARS

I have listed Alec's daily schedule of eating/nursing and sleeping habits. ***Please consult with a pediatrician!***

Birth to 1ˢᵗ Month:
Breastfeeding: 8 to 10 times in 24-hour period
Sleeping: 3 to 4 hour chunks of time in 24-hour period.
At 2 weeks old: Try not to let baby fall asleep while nursing. Good luck it's tough!

1st Month to 2nd Month:

Breastfeeding: 7 or 8 times

Naps: Decreased from 7 to 6 naps

Night Sleep: 6 to 7 hours

We started on some sort of a schedule. Alec was nursing every 2 to 2 ½ hours: nursing 30 minutes, playing 30 minutes, then sleeping for 1 ½ hours.

8 weeks to 10 weeks:

Breastfeeding: 6 times

Naps: 5

Night Sleep: Increased from 8 to 9 hours

We did the "crying it out" when Alec was nine weeks old. It took two nights.

Alec was waking up between 6:00am - 7:00am.

Here is an example of Alec's schedule at **nine weeks old:**

Wake-up @ 6:00am - 6 feedings and 5 naps per day

EAT	SLEEP
6:00am	7:45am
9:15am	11:00am
12:30pm	2:15pm
3:45pm	5:30pm
7:00pm	8:30pm
9:30pm	10:00pm (bedtime)

Wake-up @ 7:00am - 6 feedings and 5 naps per day

EAT	SLEEP
7:00am	8:30am
10:00am/10:30am	11:30am

1:00pm	2:30pm
4:00pm	5:30pm
7:00pm/7:30pm	8:30pm/9:00pm
9:30pm	10:00pm (bedtime)

10 weeks:

Breastfeeding: 6 times

Naps: 4

Night Sleep: 9 to 10 hours

Alec was getting about 14 hours of sleep in 24-hour period.

12 weeks (3 months) to 4 months:

Breastfeeding: 7 times

Naps: 3 and then decreased to 2 naps a day at 3 ½ months

Night Sleep: 10 - 12 hours

Nursing times: 7:00am, 9:00am, 11:15am, 1:15pm, 4:00pm, 7:15pm, 8:15pm

Alec was getting about 14 hours of sleep in 24-hour period.

4 months to 5 months:

Breastfeeding: 7 times

Naps: 2 (1 ½ to 2 ½ hours each)

Night Sleep: 11 hours

5 months to 6 months:

Breastfeeding: 7 times

Naps: 2 (1 ½ to 2 ½ hours each)

Night Sleep: 10 or 11 hours

I got Alec down to nursing 20 minutes instead of 30 minutes.

6 months to 7 months:
Breastfeeding: 6
Naps: 2 (1 ½ to 2 ½ hours each)
Night Sleep: 10 ½ hours
I would have started Alec on eating solids, but we were traveling for three weeks in the States.

7 months to 8 months:
Breastfeeding/Milk Formula: 5 times, along with eating solids
Naps: 2 (1 ½ to 2 ½ hours each)
Night Sleep: 11 hours
I started Alec on pureed vegetables and introduced water in a sippy cup. And I began to give him milk formula from a bottle. I stopped breastfeeding completely when Alek turned eight months so, it took one month to wean him off completely. Instead of bedtime at 8-8:30pm, changed to 7:30-7:45pm. Waking around 6:30-7am. Alek's 2 naps @ 9:30am and 1:30pm.

8 months to 9 months:
Milk Formula and Solids: 6 bottles and eating 2 meals (lunch and dinner)
Naps: 2 (1 ½ to 2 hours each)
Night Sleep: 11 hours

9 months to 13 months:
Milk Formula and Solids: 3 bottles and eating 3 meals (breakfast, lunch and dinner)
Naps: 2 (1 ½ to 2 hours each)
Night Sleep: 11 hours

13 months to 23 months:

Milk Formula and Solids: 2 bottles and eating 3 meals

Naps: 1 (2 to 2 ½ hours)

Night Sleep: 11 hours

We had to adjust Alec's naps to the daycare schedule. They changed to noon - 2pm.

16 months:

Milk Formula and Solids: 1 bottle and eating 3 meals and small snack

23 months:

No more milk formula/bottle

* Be aware of Sleep Regression at this age

2 years to 2 ½ half years:

Solids: 3 meals and snack

Naps: 1 (2 hours)

Night Sleep: 11 hours

2 ½ half years to 3 years:

Solids: 3 meals and snack

Naps: 1 (1 ½ hours)

Night Sleep: 10 hours

Wake-up: 6:00am

Bedtime: 7:30pm (falls asleep between 7:45pm & 8:00pm)

3 years to 4 years:

Depending on your child's daycare schedule will determine the sleeping schedule!

When Alec took a 1 ½ hours nap then bed time was around 8:30pm. If he didn't take a nap, we changed his bed time to 7:00/7:30pm. And sometimes even 6:30pm if he had a very active day. With his daycare's holiday breaks and the weekends, it was hit-or-miss with naps. When he was almost four, there was no need for a nap except for extremely active days, and he would only fall asleep in the car.

* Sleep Regression

A heads up that your little darling might undergo *sleep regression*. This type of sleep behavior is not associated with cutting teeth. That's another beast in itself. This is the type when your child wakes up at 4am in the morning, bright-eyed and bushy-tailed. Or they wake up at midnight and play till 5am and then fall back to sleep; resulting in no daycare that day. Argh!

When Alec was twenty-two months old sleep regression set in, and it lasted almost three months. The age and length of time varies. A friend son's sleep regression started when he was one and a half and lasted close to five months.

Jens thinks sleep regression is due to full moons. I'm sorry but no. Not all kids go through it but a larger percentage do. It seems to me more boys than girls.

One mom posted in a mother's Facebook group about a sleep setback. Instantly, there was a long thread of comments telling of the exact same sleeping problems with their children. Interestingly, that only a few mentioned 'sleep regression'.

I would advise not to drop the daytime nap. I have spoken to many moms and read online forums explaining how it doesn't help. We tried a few of times and didn't help. And at this age, children's bodies are too small and need to recharge with a nap. Also, stick to the regularly scheduled bedtime.

Sleep regression is tough on toddlers, but this one is definitely tougher on parents. As a parent, I think the best thing to say to a parent whose child is going through this tiresome, sleeping pattern is simply, "It's not your fault." Sometimes things are out of our control. They are not doing this on purpose. Stay strong and give unconditional love to your little ones.

I do have one strong piece of advice. When your little darling (Gremlin at these god-forsaken-hours) is wide awake during this time, parents should become the boring-est people ever. Do not talk to your child. Do not play with your child. Just sit on the floor (or lay) motionless while the Gremlin plays happily away completely oblivious to this most damnable, heinous, atrocious time.

WONDERFUL WORLD OF THE GERMAN HEALTHCARE SYSTEM

I am awestruck that the German healthcare system pays one hundred percent of the cost for a midwife. Everyone is allowed a midwife in Germany - first or fifth baby - doesn't matter. In fact, a midwife must be present at the birth. During my labor, there was a doctor, two midwives and Jens. In Germany, most husbands stay throughout all the stages of labor.

One remarkable service the German healthcare system provides are home visits. Midwives always come to the home! For free! No extra cost! About three months before Alec's due date, mine came for a home visit. We went over all my questions to help me prepare for his arrival. It was also beneficial for her to see our setup at home for any safety issues, for example, she didn't approve of the crib padding. A nurse or doctor in the States would have never been able to catch that. Also, she explained about what *stuff* we needed and didn't need.

Besides going to my doctor for ultra-sounds, my midwife came to our home for all the other pre-labor checkups; about five visits. After the birth when you return home from the hospital, the midwife will come every day or every other day the first week and then a few more home appointments. They weigh and perform thorough checkups on the baby and mother.

I was also surprised to learn - that besides pregnancies - a lot of doctors still do home visits on request. The Germans think, "Hey, if you are sick and not feeling well…why would you want to leave your house? And you end up spreading all the germs around and getting everyone else sick." Of course this doesn't happen regularly, but in special circumstances, one may request it.

After a phone consultation, our pediatrician thought Alec might have whooping cough so, she came to our home that evening and made a sample to see if he had it; turns out he didn't. But it was incredible that she visited us. I would have hated to take Alec in the middle of winter to the doctor's office while putting others at risk. He could have caught something else in the waiting room, too.

I'm not a cheerleader for the whole medical system here. I had unpleasant experiences. Because of Alec's head size, I had to be induced. Being induced can be more painful and result in a longer delivery. I knew going in that I wanted an epidural, but the pain was so excruciating that the doctors gave me too much, and I could not help with any of the pushing. The doctor had to use a vacuum to get Alec out. Also, inducing labor might still result in a cesarean delivery. Many women I know experienced this: getting induced, suffering many hours - sometimes days - of labor, and then having an emergency cesarean. In addition, I did not heal well from the surgical incision (Perineotomy/Episiotomy).

But I told the nurses and doctors that I wanted to have a vaginal birth. I read too much about how cesarean births are more difficult to recover from than vaginal births. In my case, I would have preferred a C-section, however, at the time, I didn't know about the side effects/ risks of induction.

In the United States, one has the option of a 'designer birth'. It's a caesarian section and then a tummy tuck is done immediately after. It's also called a 'mommy tuck'. People shell out big bucks for these operations. I find the whole procedure ludicrous. No woman's body should be tortured like this after delivering a baby. It shows how warped, sick and twisted America's sense of beauty is towards women. The pressure to be thin, fit and tight is totally misconceived. I feel we need to re-discover what makes a woman beautiful, and it sure as hell doesn't start with a 'mommy tuck'.

Another medical mishap that I experienced was not being diagnosed with Hypothyroidism (an under active thyroid). Throughout my entire pregnancy, I was sleeping around twelve hours at night and taking two or three naps per day. I told my doctor I was tired, but she said it was from being pregnant. Then after Alec arrived, my mom said I felt tired because I was breastfeeding. Also, I felt extremely cold which is a symptom of hypothyroidism. [26] That summer, I slept in fleece pajamas with a down comforter, and I still shivered. Coldness cut to my bones, and often my body would actually shake.

It wasn't until Alec was seven months old, and my skin had turned yellow that I finally went to an internist. Jens thought I had jaundice. Nope, a thyroid problem which often onsets during pregnancy. The doctor diagnosed the problem within ten minutes and confirmed by testing my thyroid-stimulating hormone (TSH). Unfortunately, she said I will have to take medication for the rest of my life.

Overactive and underactive thyroids can cause miscarriages and low birthweight. [27] It's important to test TSH levels. There can also be a strong relation to postpartum depression. In a study, published by *The New England Journal of Medicine*, postpartum thyroid dysfunction occurs more often in women with depression than women without. [28]

I also suffered from pelvic pain from the combination of the weight of Alec on my pelvic floor muscles throughout the pregnancy and my Perineotomy/Episiotomy - the surgical tear "can lead to so much pain, discomfort, and limitations of functioning" from the tightness. [29] For these exact reasons, in France, it is "custom for every woman who goes through a vaginal delivery to see a physical therapist as part of her postpartum treatment." [30]

I went to countless appointments to my OB/GYN before giving up on her. I went to physical therapy - even one specializing in pelvic-floor muscles. I saw a few more doctors and read way too much online to scare me into believing I had cancer. I don't recommend self-diagnosis via the internet but what else does one have after multiple trips to multiple doctors?

I finally stumbled upon an OB/GYN that understood my chronic pain. I mentioned Secondary Vaginismus, pelvic-floor dysfunction, and a surgery called Vestibulecyomy. He said *slow down*. After he calmed me down, we discussed my pain, and he did a quick examination. He prescribed me OeKolp-Creme. In one month, the pain subsided by half. After two more months, I was practically pain free.

"The National Institutes for Health notes that one in four American women suffers from a pelvic-floor issue at some point in her life." [31] Sadly, it goes untreated and most women just live with the pain. But how can this many women have this problem, and there is so little awareness in the medical field!? It took me almost *two years* to find a doctor that cured me. My new and improved OB/GYN explained that not enough doctors know about chronic pelvic pain (CCP) and how to treat each case. And a lot of doctors say that it is *all in one's head.* Wrong! If you suffer from this kind of pain keep searching for a doctor that has experience in treatment or can recommend a specialist.

In extreme cases, a doctor will surgically remove nerve endings. It's a minor procedure called a Vestibulecyomy. I was at my whits' end that I almost had the surgery but luckily the creme worked for my musculoskeletal disorder - "range from bones being out of alignment to muscles feeling knotted, tight, tired, or weak to nerve irritation." [32]

My unfortunate medical/doctor experiences could have happened in the States as well. One has to be proactive and keep searching for a doctor that is knowledgeable with the problem in order to receive the correct diagnosis. In order to figure out the health problem, it's ok to start with the internet but, in addition, read books and talk to physicians as soon as possible.

COMING TO AMERICA

"Your baby is the best one I have ever had on a flight," Lufthansa flight attendant. Alec had slept ten hours! It did help that he was able to sleep in a baby bassinet provided by the airline. Jens and I had counted it as our first date night. It wasn't exactly a romantic evening, but we got to choose our own movies; a win-win situation.

And as passengers exited the airplane, they gave us approving nods. They were pleased that Alec didn't cry and howl throughout the flight. Everyone was a happy camper!

We landed at Dallas/Fort Worth Airport and had to travel another four hours by car to get to my parent's house - located outside a teensy tiny Texas town. But not before we had to wait in the U.S. customs line. It was looking like at least an hour wait; not fun with a six-month-old baby.

There was no getting around it until we teamed up with a Russian mom and her toddler. We were standing in line together and complaining how there wasn't some sort of special assistance line for senior citizens or families with young children and babies. We flagged down a couple of airport service assistants, but they wouldn't allow us to go to the front the line. I had given up, but the Russian was relentless. Finally, one assistant (a mom) escorted all of us up to the front.

Luckily, we didn't get held up in customs like Jens did when he traveled through Kansas on a business trip. They stopped and questioned him regarding Kinder Surprise Eggs. Kinder Eggs are made of a hollow chocolate shell and a small toy inside. They are illegal in the United States. Never mind if he had any weapons or bombs; they questioned him if he was smuggling any Kinder Eggs.

Other weapon related issues we have to deal with while traveling in my home state of Texas are guns. Before staying at my relatives' homes, I kindly ask them to lock up all guns in the house. And on our second trip to the States when Alec was two years old, I asked that no violent video games be played in his presence. I envisioned their eyes rolling but everyone complied and surprisingly with no back lash.

Driving around in central Texas, it doesn't take long to recognize that German immigrants settled in this area - starting in the 1830's. The Texas road signs display the German town/city names: New Braunfels, Fredricksburg, Luckenbach, Bergheim, Boerne, Muenster, Schulenburg, Weimar, Shiner. And the two cities I grew up near

Walburg and Pflugerville. This is sometimes referred to as the German Belt. They - like many immigrants still today - were seeking prosperity and religious liberty. There were also many Czech descendants moving into Texas as well.

The funny thing about these city names; me and most of the rest of the Texas population have been pronouncing them all wrong. With Jens in the drivers seat, he would point out and say the German town names on the highway signs. The first couple of times, I corrected him. But soon realized, to my embarrassment, he was correcting me. This continued to the last names of my friends that I grew up with. Apparently, my friends have been mispronouncing their last names, too.

BREASTFEEDING IN PUBLIC

Despite the heavy price tag of shipping a package overseas, we received some thoughtful baby gifts that were useful for our trip to the States. Two particularly were very thoughtful that I would like to point out. The first was alcohol testing-strips for breast feeding moms who occasionally like to have a glass of wine after a very exhausting day. These strips analyze the breastmilk and will show if alcohol is present or not; determining if one should 'pump and dump'. I should have bought ten dozen boxes because my German mom-friends have never heard of them, and they all agreed they would buy them if on the market. I'm adding these alcohol strips to my list of U.S. import ideas.

The other gift was perfect for our trip to the States: the Hooter Hider, quite popular in Texas. My cousin Rebecca sent it to me. It's a nursing cover so, moms can discreetly nurse their babies in public and perhaps even at home. It's conservative in the Bible Belt.

I used it a couple of times in Hamburg when we had dinner with friends, but it was more of a nuisance. When a baby is ready to nurse. They are ready…now! When you have a baby wailing for their milk and a mom is digging around for the Hooter Hider, things tend to get more than hysterical. If a mom has to put on the Hooter Hider while holding the frenzied baby; forget it. The baby is flapping its arms everywhere, head twisting and turning, and you lose the baby in the fabric. It's basically a camping tent.

Maybe I started the whole cover thing too late. When Alec would nurse with the cover, he would play with the fabric, and he would pull it into his face. Then he would latch off and more crying. I would wrestle with the fabric to find Alec's face for him to latch on again; all the time my boob was exposed.

In Germany, women don't use floral-printed nursing covers. One just whips it out and gets going. But if they wear a nursing bra and turn slightly away from viewing, people can't see anything. Truthfully, it isn't a big deal. The first time I nursed in public, in Germany, I was nervous…for the first ten seconds. Not until I traveled back to the States did I realize how stressful, inconvenient and shameful it can be to nurse in public.

When traveling, one usually eats out at restaurants. Until we did our big first family vacation in the States, I never grasped the reason for the occasional chair in a woman's bathroom. I thought, you go into a bathroom and sit on a toilet. What's the chair for? Here's the answer; for nursing. So many mothers get shunned from the table that they go to the bathroom to nurse their baby. In most cases, there is no chair so, mother's go into a toilet stall to breastfeed!

While visiting one of my brother's in southern California, my niece and I went shopping at an outdoor mall. It came time to nurse Alec, and I found the closest bench. I can not tell you how many dirty looks

I got! I asked my niece if she minded and she said *no*. But after a few more minutes, a mom and her two young girls walked by. The mom gasped, grabbed her girls' hands and sped away. What was going on? I quickly looked down to check out Alec and my boobs. I was completely covered up. You couldn't see anything! I asked my niece if she wanted to go. She said, "Well, maybe we should go." This is exactly what I didn't want to happen. Society had judged me, and we were shamed to go to the bathroom. Luckily there was a restroom nearby, but a few minutes walk feels like eternity with a screaming hungry baby.

I find America's view on breastfeeding in public immensely hypocritical. Women's breasts are all over the place: T.V., movies, advertisements, fashion. Women and girls walking down the street in tight tops or revealing cleavage is far more inappropriate than a square inch of my nursing bra showing.

And what about all the boob implants? That plastic stretches from the East to the West coast and into the conservative South. And it my astonishment, the "Mormon corridor" in Utah. Yes, boob jobs are popular amongst Mormons. I find it hard to accept that a mother can be criticized for breastfeeding their precious, angelic baby while boobs are all over prime-time public television. People are so use to the unnatural that we have forgotten what the natural is meant for.

Even in countries where women have to dress conservatively, it is acceptable for women to breastfeed modestly covered in public. You won't believe the countries I am referring to...hold onto your miniskirts: Ghana, Kenya, Uganda, Zambia, Bangladesh, Sri Lanka, Nepal, India, Pakistan, Iran, and parts of Afghanistan. [33] Yes, folks, these extremely religious countries have Americans beat on publicly nursing babies. Pathetic. It's ok to breastfeed in Pakistan but not the

U.S.?! Totally acceptable in parts of Afghanistan but glares and stares in the UK?!

But, I admit, sometimes things are taken a little too far in the opposite direction. Take for example in one of my free German conversation meet-ups. They are organized by the German government and held at public libraries. Our local library is a ten-minute bike ride from our house. There are usually about eight people, and we sit around a small, round table touching elbows conversing in broken German.

One lesson there was a teacher assistant helping out, and she had her eight month old baby with her. The baby quickly became hungry, and she began to nurse her at our crowded table. Ok, fine, no problem. But the entire time, the baby was latching on and off every twenty or thirty seconds. And when the baby would latch off, the mother would not cover up. Her entire boob/nipple was staring at everyone until the baby decided to go back on. This occurred on and off the hour lesson.

Keep in mind that everyone was there to learn German so, that means no one at the table is German. And no one shared this cultural trait at this greatly diverse table. For example, there was a sixty year old guy from Iran, an even older dude from England, and a young guy from the U.S.A. If I was in shock, undoubtedly they were, too. Needless to say, I never saw any of them again at "Dialog in Deutsch."

That evening I told Jens the story. Nonchalantly he responded, "Well, how else is she suppose to feed her baby?" Gosh, what a German I married.

THE TERRIFIC TWOS

Undoubtedly, our efforts towards sleep training and a proper diet have been the foundation of a happy child, and selfishly, our sanity.

Structure, boundaries and routines has made Alec blossom. The wonder and excitement these little creatures express makes for terrific twos not the terrible twos.

We had a friend over for dinner one night, and it was time for Alec's bedtime routine. After brushing his teeth and reading a book, Alec said *nighty night* to our guest, and I led him to his bedroom. We quickly went over his day. I usually ask him what he remembers eating, the best part of his day, and I might praise him of a certain action, for example, he helped a friend get-up who fell at the playground. Starting at the age of three, I would remind him more of his good behavior since it's a more volatile age for misbehaving. [34]

I returned a few minutes later to our guest.

"That's it?" he said.

"That's what?" I said.

"Alec is in bed?" he said.

"Yeah, why?" I said.

"I usually have to spend half an hour with my girls" he said.

By age two, Alec has become mama's little helper. He loves to load and unload the dishwasher and the washing machine. He follows me around with a paper towel; ready to clean any spots that I missed. Before bed, we put away all his books and toys while singing the clean-up song. I made up the song. It's a pretty pathetic song, but at least he knows what to do.

Also, Alec took a strong interest in wanting to help cook. At some point, my mom planted in my head how important it is to cook with your child. We get a kick out of Alec helping us for pizza night. I buy ready made pizza dough and roll it out. Alec smears the sauce, sprinkles the cheese, and I try to help him properly distribute the extra bits like pineapple or ham.

And about two years of age, Alec has almost mastered counting to ten in German and English. He even counts with his fingers the proper way depending on the language. Germans start with their thumb for number one. In the States, the number one is with the pointer finger. I began to teach Alec numbers by using raisins and sesame pretzel sticks. And I would also ask him, "Do you want two or three pretzels?" Alec would respond, "Tree, mama!"

And by this age, I've realized we have raised a more cautious child compared to other kids. Partly because every other word out of my mouth is *be careful*. We try to make a conscience effort not to yell at Alec, but when something is dangerous, my mama-lion instinct kicks in with a strong *no* and often *are you crazy?!* Then he receives a lengthy, adult-comprehensible explanation of why he can hurt himself.

Pre-toddlers naturally act out because they don't know right from wrong, but at the age two, they have the capacity to know why it is wrong. [35] It's now up to the parents/caretakers to explain the why and attend to any repeated actions. And instruct your toddler to do something; it's not the time for suggestions. [36]

TOP TEN ALEC FREAK-OUTS AS A TWO YEAR OLD

When I...
> roll up his sleeves.
> peel his banana more than half way.
> cut his bread in pieces.
> don't leave enough room on a cracker for him to
> hold without touching the spread.
> flush the toilet for him.
> turn off the light for him.
> gave him socks and underwear as Christmas presents.

don't take off the 'strings' on the banana.
don't let him peel the yogurt lid off.

When one of my hairs is laying on one of his toys, his finger, on his shirt, anywhere. Actually, anything to do with one of my hairs is a complete freak-out; however, he loves the hair that is attached to my head.

MOST ADORABLE ALEC MOMENT

He ate his banana. He asked for more banana. I told him he already ate his banana, and it was in his stomach. He lifted his shirt looking for the banana.

Chapter 3

Parenting and Food
Teaching your Child to Eat

MILK FORMULA

One of my strongest opinions when it comes to a new learning experience, especially with food and drink, is to always start with the healthiest habit. If you don't want your kids to demand apple juice at mealtimes, then only serve water from the very beginning. One must remember that babies have never tasted anything but milk. If a parent never introduced ice cream, then a child would never ask for ice cream. If a parent never gave ham to their child, then they would never say, "I want a ham sandwich for lunch." Anything a child requests to eat is because they had that certain food at some point in their life.

They are starving for nutrients. Their little bodies need energy to play and grow. Babies and toddlers crave a well-balanced nourishing meal that consists of proteins, vegetables, healthy starches and fruit offered as snacks or desserts.

Of course milk should also be given a lot of thought and attention.

When I stopped breastfeeding Alec, I had many questions that I asked my pediatrician. She gave a lot of guidance regarding what to look for when buying Alec's formula. She did not tell me a specific brand but advised us to buy organic and to stay away from the big conventional food brands.

Jens and I did our own research and through Oko-Test (a German consumer magazine). We found Alec's infant formula *Holle Bio-Anfangsmilch*. It is organic through biodynamic farming. Alec loved the taste, and he had no health problems. While researching this formula, I stumbled upon a long list (American's love lists) of other positive reasons to choose this brand of formula, for example, the cows are treated humanely - no dehorning and the cows graze on biodynamic lawns. And I couldn't believe it is cheaper than the leading brand milks! And perhaps more importantly, the first ingredient is skim milk rather than whey powder.

One of my friends in the U.S. had an unfortunate experience of discovering her formula's first ingredient was corn syrup. This is her email to me - word for word. I think many moms can identify with her story:

Ok so get this. Sadly I am no longer breast feeding. I was trying SO hard, but with going back to work - even pumping 2x a day while I'm here, it was just not good enough and I stopped producing milk. If I ever had another baby (which I'm not), I would take 3 extra months off, unpaid just to breast feed. I felt so sad mixing the baby a bottle of chemicals to drink. So XXX Brand, out of no where, because I never gave them my address, sends all of these products to your home right after you deliver. They even send this book that talks about how great breast feeding is, this is top choice, these are the benefits, definitely do it, hooray, hoorah, etc, HOWEVER, when you stop you should use our brand. So the day came when I had to start supplementing, but I didn't feel too bad at first because he was still drinking mostly breast milk. But as I dried up and the table turned, he was drinking mostly formula and only 2 bottles of breast milk. As my bad feelings and guilt about it began to increase, I thought it was finally time to come out of denial and check the ingredient label. I look on the back ingredient label to see what's in it and guess what the first ingredient was.............................CORN SYRUP. It was so heart breaking and it's just gross!!! It smells, gives him gas, and his poop smells toxic - it NEVER use to smell with my milk. Can you imagine? So after weeks of feeding him this, I just found another brand that's "organic". Corn syrup is listed as the 4th or 5th ingredient instead - this is organic in this country. You are so lucky to live in a place that actually cares!!

Ever wonder why you receive free baby formula via the post mail? Because by an international health policy, companies are not allowed to advertise infant formula even in America. Oh, you thought they were giving you free formula out of the goodness of their hearts? Not a chance. And by law, they are not even allowed to have coupons, for example, cut-out coupons in the advertising section of the newspaper.

Almost all tobacco advertising is illegal in the U.S. as well. How is this related to infant formula? Governments finally realized the power of advertising and marketing; by how they can take advantage and manipulate consumers. Duh!

And why are there laws to ban formula? Because law makers know that breast milk is the most important nourishment for food/drink. And no companies should promote any substitute over breast milk. Sadly the U.S. has one of the lowest rates of breastfeeding because it's difficult to combine breast feeding/pumping with work. [1]

Our pediatrician also advised us on how much milk Alec should drink until he turns two. It is the same for normal children, but formulas can have some slight variations so, it's important to discuss with your doctor. She did warn that too much milk is not good because the child will not be as hungry and interested in their lunch or dinner. Hello! Yes! But many parents don't seem to grasp this simple piece of common sense.

THE FRENCH WAY

I think the French do a superb job with starting babies with healthy eating habits that leads to eating a wide variety of food. French children have a reputation for eating adult food. And why do French children eat so well? Parents start them out on vegetables; no rice cereals or grains. [2] And no fruit juices - only water in addition to their milk. As they get older, French kids are allowed to drink juice at breakfast or with their afternoon snack; water with lunch and dinner. [3]

I was shocked to read in many American parenting books to start with cereals. [4, 5] Or one leading expert recommends to start with pears. [6] What baby is going to like a vegetable after eating a sweet pear?

I left out many bland vegetables in the beginning. Instead of purée potatoes, Alec got sweet potatoes. I steamed peas, pumpkin, spinach, eggplant, zucchini and many more for him to discover a variety of flavors. And he ate them! All of them! He still continues to happily chomp away on these wonderful vitamin-packed vegetables. One of his favorites is avocado. I am convinced he loves them because I always joke that he is made of avocados. I ate them throughout my entire pregnancy along with chicken fried sandwiches and burritos.

Later I learned about how different foods release sugar faster than others by their glycemic index. The faster the sugar releases, the faster the baby gets hungry. For example, sweet potatoes and carrots release sugar slowly keeping the baby full for a longer period of time but pumpkin and rice have a high glycemic index which releases it too quickly. So, it's smart to avoid foods that have a high glycemic index at dinner time. [7]

When I first started making Alec's food at seven months, I painstakingly prepared all his food. It wasn't difficult making the food, but it sure took a lot more time and energy rather than simply buying jars from the grocery store.

In hindsight, I should have bought a recipe book for babies; however, the result was tasting foods separately. It's not beneficial to mask flavors every meal. Even babies should know what individual vegetables taste like. Instead, I was pulling information on how to prepare meals for babies from everywhere: blogs, my mother, friends. Compiling all this material and testing different foods was the hardest part. For example, avocados don't freeze. They freeze, but, when unfrozen, they're pretty revolting. Potatoes don't freeze well either so, as a bit of a time saver, I would add instant potatoes as a filler with other foods when Alec turned one.

My mother suggested to start out with purée carrots. A fun, bright vegetable loaded with Vitamin A. They have a slightly sweet taste that is a good base to mix-in later with not so great tasting vegetables. My cousin makes a fiery salsa dip but with a snippet of a sweet taste. Everyone thinks he adds honey; nope, purée carrots.

The first time my husband and I fed Alec it was incredibly disappointing. 98% of my painstakingly prepared, non G.M.O., non chemically treated carrots were everywhere but in his tummy! Of course we laughed it off and took some hilarious photos.

More than the first few times of feeding Alec, the precious carrots ended up in his hair, nose, ears, in between his toes, chair, wall, floor, and I was completely smeared with them, too. It took more than a week for Alec to understand that those carrots were going in his belly. Jens and I never gave in and fed him *brei* (infant cereal).

The translation is infant cereal that is dehydrated rice or mixed grains that you add hot water or baby formula. I strongly encourage parents not to start with *brei*. Later on, introducing vegetables will make for many fussy fits in the high chair and a lot of *no's* and *nein's*. It's mind boggling that after the first or second time of a baby refusing to eat vegetables parents quickly switch to fruit or a carbohydrate.

This also includes juices! Please start your baby with water. I spoke to a few moms whose baby wouldn't take water so, they added a touch of juice. This does not work folks. Water has a very specific taste. Even when juice is highly diluted, it's a different taste. Period. Yes, fruit juice has nutritional value, but getting your child use to the taste of water and requesting it is far more important at this young age. Going from water to fruit juice is a lot easier than vice versa. My friend's daughter refused to drink water until she was two years old because the parents started with mixing apple juice and water. Fruits are fine but not as juice at this stage. In addition, even diluted juice will lead to tooth decay from the acidity and sugar. [8]

Did starting Alec with carrots make him such a good lil' eater? Is this the sole answer to getting your baby to eat cauliflower, kohlrabi, squash, chickpeas, parsnip and Brussels sprouts? In addition: couscous, quinoa, soy yogurt, tofu and a variety of meat and fish. Yes, but it's also because Jens and I never gave up. And we give positive reinforcement and encouragement to Alec when it comes to meal times.

THE GERMAN WAY

From seven months to one year old, I made all of Alec's purée baby food. Since I was pregnant, I started collecting recipes via Pinterest, blogs, Facebook, books, etc. I wanted to know I was feeding my baby one hundred percent natural food. And if buying, prepping, steaming, blending and storing the baby food gave me peace of mind, then I did it. Plus, all the other German moms were busy making their darling's food, right? Maybe not.

The first place I started noticing all the prepared, packaged baby food was in the bottom of baby strollers. In Hamburg, like any other big city in Germany with fantastic public transportation, many people don't have cars. If one does have a car, other than driving to work, one seldom uses the car because they have found a good parking spot, and they don't want to lose it. Therefore, moms and dads are out shopping usually with the baby or toddler in the stroller. And most parents just throw the stuff in the bottom of the stroller because their children are screaming at the top of their lungs while everyone in line is giving them a go-to-hell look. Hence everybody sees what you purchased at the store because you didn't have time to put the groceries in your super cute, trendy, shopping bags.

To see if my assumption about parents buying store-bought baby food instead of homemade was correct, I decided to take a stroll down the baby food isle at a grocery store. I could not believe the selection and amount! There is definitely a market here for all this product to be taking up so much grocery store real estate. Not only was I finding it in the major supermarket chains but at bio (organic farming) stores like Alnatura.

But the longer I lived in Germany and understood their food standards/laws, it all made sense. German parents don't worry about what is in store bought baby food because they simply don't have to. The European Commission and German food laws are so strict when it comes to the production and selling of food products; whether it is honey, spinach, oranges, milk, meat, apple juice or processed/packaged food. Even discount supermarket chains like Aldi or Lidl have to comply with these standards.

Specifically, Germany has had a long history in understanding, practicing and abiding by certain food laws. The oldest known food law in the world comes from Germany in the sixteenth century regarding beer. Certain ingredients are only allowed in making beer. And most breweries in Germany still comply with this law.

The food laws in the U.S. are far more lenient than in the European Union. There are two main reasons why food produced in the U.S. is not allowed to be sold for consumption in the EU: genetically modified food (G.M.O.) and how U.S. cattle and other animals are treated with hormones and antibiotics. It is kind of an unbelievable statement, isn't it? The EU has deemed food from the U.S. unsafe to eat. But what can we expect from a society that buys their lunch from a vending machine?

Food labeling is another reason why many U.S. food companies can't sell their products in the EU. Makes me wonder what's in Gatorade. That's correct; Gatorade is not sold in Germany.

I grew up eating lots of fresh foods but also a ton of processed and microwavable foods. I didn't care much for American hotdogs unless cooked over a camp fire; however, I can eat s'mores anytime, day or night; microwaved or camp-fired roasted for that golden-brown-delicious (G.B.D.) taste. I picked up the slang *GBD* from Chef David

Chang on *The Mind of a Chef.*

When it comes to food and nutrition, I feel a little sense a peace and not nearly stressed out in Germany. And I think we all need less stress. But I do have to keep en eye on those expiration dates as the grocery store lady once warned me. And I have to worry about bread crumbs as the bread isn't glued together like in the United States. My grandpa use to call white bread and crackers *rat poisoning.*

If we lived in America, I would be standing next to Michelle Obama fighting the good fight against the G.O.P. (Grand Old Party AKA The Republican Party). Mrs. Obama advocated the Healthy Hunger-Free Kids Act in 2010 that promotes healthier food choices at schools. And she is very active with her "Let's Move" campaign.

Mrs. Obama is bringing attention to America's alarming rate of child obesity. The C.D.C. (Centers for Disease Control and Prevention) reported, "In 2012, more than one third of children and adolescents were overweight or obese." [9] And, in 2015, the C.D.C. published that 29.1 million people in the U.S. have diabetes. America's sugar addiction is the cause for the rise in diabetes. Many people go for years without being tested for this silent killer - 8.1 million Americans undiagnosed. [10]

One thing that does taste like more sugar here are the colas. I heard before that in different countries, they use different recipes. In Germany, they have more of a sweet taste but not so chemically. Is that a word? My tastebuds have concluded that there is more natural sugar in the EU's colas and more artificial sugars in American colas. These tend to peel the enamel off teeth.

There is a larger variety of vegetables in Germany, too. I had never seen so many types of potatoes, tomatoes and squash until browsing the local farmers markets. An unusual mix of zebra stripes, colors and shapes. Recently I bought a *Moormöhren* (type of carrot - dark orange). There is no direct English translation. Who knew that carrots are also purple, red and yellow?

The reason behind not knowing about these other types is because I have only eaten commercial vegetables. It is much cheaper to produce a smaller variety. And big U.S. food corporations demand cheap produce to make a fat profit.

My biggest concern is where Alec is getting his protein. I am not only talking about meat. I grew up eating brown pinto beans with cornbread - Texas meal. In addition to him eating eggs and beans (try to limit canned vegetables), I wanted him to get use to having tofu in his diet. It's a wonderful protein source and high in iron that can easily be hidden in sauces, smoothies or mixed in with more appetizing vegetables; however, Alec will eat tofu straight out of the package. In the U.S., I would have to pay close attention about which tofu I buy since it is made of soy, which has been genetically modified along with corn. In fact, most processed food contains soy, corn and/or wheat in America.

Even with the strict food laws in Germany, I hesitated on feeding Alec jarred baby food. There was something missing. I think since I had breastfed him until he was eight months old, it didn't feel right giving him something that wasn't the most fresh, pure vegetable. Yes, carrots are carrots, but I wanted him to have a carrot that was pulled from the earth and eaten in a couple of days. And that's what I did.

Alec did eat jarred baby food. I ain't gonna lie. When he turned one years old, I trekked to the store with my trusty city shopping cart and stocked up. I was darn tootin' proud of myself for preparing fresh meals, but I was over it just like I was over breast feeding. Of course I didn't serve it at every meal. I would also buy single vegetable baby food and mix it with my homemade meals. Then at twenty-one months old, Alec suddenly refused to eat jarred food anymore, and it was mostly whatever mama and papa ate.

GERMAN DAYCARE MENU

One thing that I don't like about the *kitas* are certain types of food they serve. All the meat and fish are usually battered and fried. They only serve meat once a week at lunch. I can't decide if that's good or bad. They do sometimes receive hard boiled eggs or deli meat at breakfast. One time they had American style cheese; the bright neon-orange "cheese." I pointed at the plastic goo and commented to the daycare workers jokingly, "This isn't cheese! You aren't allowed to eat this in Germany." This had them roaring with laughter, and it was never served again.

The food is rather monotonous as well: bell peppers, cucumbers, apples, bananas, pasta. At two different parent meetings, I suggested we pay an extra ten euro per month to have foods such as avocados, mangos and blackberries. Very few parents agreed with my idea (two parents actually out of twenty-five), and it was passed over quickly. At another parent meeting, I expressed concern how I was not satisfied with the food they were serving our children and maybe we could make some changes. Nothing major but leave out certain food items, for example, pudding, brownies and jam/jelly. One parent remarked, "Is the food so bad?" Again, the topic was swept under the rug, and the menu stayed the same.

My husband later said the parents probably didn't want to pay an extra ten euros. What?! We live in a well-off area. Rents were some of the highest in Hamburg. Our *kita* was filled with doctors, lawyers, business owners and other professionals. Jens explained that Germans feel that they shouldn't have to pay for any social services since their taxes are already so high. But an extra ten euros per month for their child's food? Really? And since we were living in Hamburg, daycare is entirely free for five hours. "It's the principle," stated Jens.

SWEET TOOTH

Of course one cannot shelter their child from ever trying sweets and greasy foods their entire life. But parents can have control the first couple years by giving their baby/toddler nutritious foods. And it might be enough time to form a child's palate A good example is a German's taste in desserts.

Germans are known for their baked goods. Their desserts look so decadent and irresistible, but they are not so sweet. I'm usually a little disappointed when I try them at a bakery. It's such a let down; such a fake-out. It could be a pastry, torte, cookie or a strudel. The only thing that I have found sweet is a sugar-glazed Berliner. It is kind of similar to a doughnut with a jelly filling.

Apparently, Easter is a very big deal in Germany. Like many other religious holidays here, the public and private schools recognize Easter with a lot of related activities. At Alec's *kita* (daycare), the parents were invited for a small party and to paint Easter eggs. I volunteered to bring cupcakes to be served with the coffee. Coffee and cake mid to late afternoon is the most essential meal for the Germans as brunch is to single city dwellers.

Whenever I make any desserts - made from a box in Germany, I always have to add extra sugar. After one trial and error, I learned their cake mixes taste more like lightly sweetened bread. And when I make brownies, I add extra chocolate. Not the semi-sweetened chocolate for cooking. I buy a regular chocolate candy bar and break it up into small pieces. If not, the brownies taste like a healthy muffin. And forget about finding ready-made icing. It doesn't exist here. I'm not sure because of the EU food laws saying that it's not safe to eat or there's not a market, but it's obsolete. My trick is to use Nutella as icing. I am sure my mother-in-law will collapse after reading this. But there's probably less sugar than frosting from a tub back in the States.

While everyone usually compliments my desserts, Germans always follow it with, "They are really sweet." With Jens, I have to leave one cupcake unfrosted for him, otherwise it remains untouched. And for brownies, I designate a corner with no extra chocolate chunks.

So, I made some homemade - from the box - cupcakes. To be on the safe side, I decided against my icing trick, but I did prepare them the American way with added sugar and chocolate, and I always add a teaspoon of Mexican vanilla. They turned out great. Of course the chef has the privilege of trying one first.

I admittedly felt pleased bringing my cupcakes to our *kita*. I sought their approval and desperately wanted to fit in. I strategically placed them on the food table out of reach from the children behind the coffee. Then I meticulously rearranged the cupcakes so, they were proportionately spaced.

Jens and I got busy painting an Easter egg with Alec which took a total of twenty-two seconds. We spent the next twenty minutes washing out the paint from our clothes, Alec's ears, and a blob in my hair – totally worth it. We enjoyed the chaotic mess with all the other moms and dads. Jens left with Alec's hand print on his pants as a souvenir.

Feeling peckish, I glanced over to the snacks. Oh my god! All my cupcakes were gone! Awesome! A big American *awesome*! I felt immensely pleased until I saw the children running around with chocolate smeared faces and half-eaten cupcakes in their small fists! Isn't it funny, when a child eats chocolate, no matter the amount, form, size, etc., chocolate ends up over their entire face? I nervously sprinted from parent to parent telling them that their child should not finish the cupcake because they have a lot of sugar in them. Every single one told me not to worry that they let their toddler/child eat cupcakes. I murmured *Oh, ok* and slithered away.

Later I would realize that for a toddler to eat a cupcake or any *German* dessert, it's ok most of the time. I'm not saying that there isn't any sugar, but the amount is drastically lower than in a typical dessert in the United States.

I praise the Germans on this aspect. Their food isn't loaded with sugar; therefore, one does not grow accustomed to the taste. This is exactly the case with my husband.

But I do have a sweet tooth I inherited from my mother and only European chocolate bars or truffles can satisfy it. In the bakeries, the German pastries and desserts look so mouth watering, but for my palate, they are not sweet enough.

Also when parents send their kids to a birthday party in Germany, they don't worry about the cake. You don't hear from the birthday boy's mom, "I substituted the sugar with apple sauce, and they are gluten-free." But I am proud that I came up with a moist, sugar free dessert for one of Alec's birthdays. I tweaked a few banana muffin recipes (see Appendix for recipe). Additionally, I decorated the muffins with a beach scene. I stuck cocktail umbrellas in the them and had gummy bears sunbathing next to the water (dyed, blue cream cheese). I was a Pinterest mom that day!

A BRITISH AFFAIR

One gray and rainy afternoon - which are many in Hamburg, Alec and I were invited to a playdate from an expat mother. It was a British mom's birthday, and she brought the most brilliant gin and tonic cake. Not that I have ever eaten a gin and tonic cake before, but the cake definitely did not come from a box mix. She also brought along a plate of brownies for the children. Being that she wasn't German, I wasn't too sure how sweet the Brits make their desserts.

"Are these kid friendly?" I asked.

"What do you mean?" she politely replied.

"Are they sugar-free?" I inquired ever so gently.

"Well, the brownies are alcohol-free, so, yeah, I guess they're kid friendly," she answered, taking the piss.

She must think I'm a total tosser - nutter - daft cow - knob head - plonker - bugger. I think she is the dog's bollocks, and I am gobsmacked over the delicious nosh. Here I go asking a cock-up question about the brownies. Blimey!

Thank goodness the host wasn't serving tea that afternoon or else I could have made another arse-over-tit mistake. I would have pulled my stunt of putting a splash of fruit juice in my tea. I did this one time in front of another group of English ladiez', and their eyeballs popped out of their sockets.

"What are you doing?" in a high-pitched posh accent.

I calmly calmed her from a seizure and tried to explain how good it is to add a little juice to tea. I received disapproving looks from the round table. I tried again to make my argument. Nope. They weren't having it. *Gosh, why can't I ever stop talking?*

I had broken a cultural law which can be more dangerous and

threatening. I didn't mean to be impolite or disrespectful, I was just doing what Americans do best: bastardizing food and drink.

I told my Welsh friend what happened. She was surprised that anyone said anything at all. Apparently, it's quite British to keep one's mouth shut. I could never be British.

EUREKA!

When Alec was about two years old, I was out of his plain, mild, 3.8% fat yogurt and couldn't find a suitable substitute for breakfast. I looked in our breadbox, and Jens' heavy, black bread stared back at me. Ugh, it tastes disgusting - according to this American. It's called *Das volle korn ohne konservierungs-stoffe* (the whole grain – without preservatives).

I thought there was no way Alec was going to eat this. I spread goat cheese on the dense bread. The bread package's size and weight is an exact replica of a brick. A few months later, I caught Alec using it as a step stool to reach the counter top. But sure enough, he ate it. I began thinking about all the different German breads. Most, unlike American, have more fiber and aren't made with as many refined ingredients.

In addition, one has to constantly check the ingredients on the packaging in America. I find it ironic that the food label is titled, "Nutrition Facts." Instead it should be a warning label.

Later that day, I saw a child on the playground eating a *brötchen*. I suddenly realized that I had misjudged the German parents. I had been criticizing them for giving their children bread rolls as empty, nutrition-less snacks.

In America, a bread roll would be good till the end of the week with all the preservatives and no telling what else. But in Germany, bread rolls from the bakeries have to be eaten the same day. Even something as simple as a roll can lead to a negative assumption about a group of people.

Cultural misunderstandings happen constantly. It's difficult to fully understand any cultural trait until one learns the background information and even experiences it themselves. In the field of Anthropology, this is known as an ethnographic approach. And one doesn't have to be a field researcher living in New Guinea to come across cultural differences. As our world is getting smaller, it's imperative for cultural comprehension on all levels. How many lives have been taken in countless wars fought over cultural differences?

We don't have to practice each other's cultures; however, we should be willing to respect them. It starts with education and being open-minded.

THE WORLD MARKET

There are so many clever gadgets to buy for babies and toddlers these days. One of my aunts had bought Alec a little baby feeder. It's perfect for babies beginning around six months. You drop a little piece of fruit or vegetable in the container. The baby can only chew and suck the juice out through the mesh material. This prevents choking on the skin/peel and not being able to take big bites. Genius!

So, a couple of months later, I'm watching this documentary called *Babies*. It's about babies from birth to the first year around the globe. It follows four babies from Japan, the U.S., Namibia and Mongolia. There is a scene where the baby from Mongolia is chewing and sucking on a piece of meat but not able to swallow it whole. It's the same concept as the gizmo that I described above. But the difference is that the mother (or father) did not buy it at Target. This family lives in a in a rural, remote area of Mongolia. One could assume that *stuff* is hard to come by. What one of the parents had done was stuck a toothpick through the meat. There was about a half a inch of toothpick sticking out on each side. The ends of the toothpick were resting on the baby's lips and chin while a little of the meat was hanging into their mouth. The baby was laying on its back and wrapped up with a blanket not able to swipe the meat but chew on it. Genius!

I'm not saying the devices are identical. I'm sure the F.D.A. (U.S. Food and Drug Administration) would not approve of the Mongolian fun, food taster. But it made me realize how so many things in parenting are parallel all over the world, for example, the baby food taster. In the U.S., there is a market for this type of product because parents want their children to be able to try and experience new flavors without harming their baby. I can assure you the Mongolian family has not set one foot inside a Target and has never seen a plastic feeding device with special F.D.A. approved mesh material; however, they created there own version unquestionably long before the plastic prototype.

REVISITING MILK

I'm going through my morning ritual of checking Yahoo news and see a picture of Christie Brinkley frolicking around in the Caribbean. The title reads "Christie Brinkley Shows Off Amazing Bikini Bod at 60." I choke on my coffee, and it shoots straight up my nose. When did she turn 60?! And how the hell does she look so damn good?!

I put down my coffee, got a tissue and did not skim the article. Ok, what's your secret, Christie? Vegetarian…blah, blah, blah…ok, ok. Then two words popped off the page: goat and sheep. Miss Brinkley does not eat or drink any dairy except goat and sheep.

One of Alec's doctors also recommended that he stop drinking cow milk! We had taken Alec to several doctors looking for a cure for his coughing fits at night along with his clogged ears and runny nose. Alec was "that kid" at our daycare and play groups with the constant runny nose. But before we opted for the ear tube surgery to clear all his congestion, Jens and I went for a last opinion to a highly recommended osteopath. At the time, Alec was about twenty months.

"Does he drink cow milk?" asked the doctor.

"Uh, yeah. What other milk would he drink?" me.

"There's many other alternatives. My children only drink almond and goat milk," doctor.

"There's no way Alec is going to give up cow's milk and drink... *goat milk*," me.

"I guarantee you will see a big improvement with him," doctor.

"But Alec isn't lactose intolerant. He doesn't get sick from drinking milk," me.

"It's not about being lactose intolerant," doctor.

"I don't understand. What's wrong with cow milk?" me letting out a big sigh.

The osteopathic doctor went on to explain how cow milk is very complex compared to other animal milk and nut/soy milk. It's hard to digest (more acidic and irritating the intestines). He said it was fine for him to even drink horse milk but absolutely no cow's milk. After hearing enough about how humans can not break down cow proteins and something about the genetic makeup and health effects, I went out and bought two different types of almond milk. Sorry, I didn't like the idea of Alec consuming horse milk. The almond was a no-go for Alec. I couldn't stand it either. Not even in my coffee.

Next we tried goat milk. First, I took a sip of the goat milk. Blah! I dove over the kitchen sink, and my gag reflexes kicked in. There was no way in Alec was going to drink that. But he did. He sucked it down so fast! He loved it! I. Could. Not. Believe. It.

I can gorge on goat cheese omelettes and saganaki (Greek fried sheep cheese). But goat milk?! Alec didn't blink an eyelash with the different taste. I still can't get over how much he likes goat milk and other alternative cow dairy products like goat or soy yogurt.

After three days of cow-free dairy, Alec's coughing was cut in half; by the fourth night, totally gone. He had suffered three straight months of coughing every single night, and everyone brushed it off as "the *kita* cough". We had tried every coughing syrup on the grocery shelf and in the *Reformhaus* (health food store), but nothing had worked except completely eliminating cow milk and cow dairy products from his diet. Poof! Gone! Goat milk really does a body good.

Update: Alec is four years old. He still only drinks goat milk. He eats goat and sheep cheese. As for yogurt, soy to balance it out. He does not eat or drink any cow dairy. Of course there are exceptions: at a restaurant or when eating pizza; however, if I make homemade pizza, he gets goat cheese. But absolutely no glasses of cow milk.

In the United States, cow dairy is a big business. In 2012, the U.S. Census of Agriculture reported 35.5 billion dollars in sales. [11] And just how important is milk? Profitable enough for Coca-Cola to get involved. Yes, the sugar, super-power house is now in the milk business named Fairlife, and it's almost double the price of regular milk. [12]

Internet research on "why cow dairy is bad for you" will take you on a labyrinthine surf ride. But my favorite argument (statement) is from Steve Jobs. I ran across this nugget while trying to find advertising/marketing tips for my book. In 1997, Jobs was giving an internal talk at Apple regarding marketing and rolling out the new ad campaign *Think Different*. He mentioned (cow) milk because of their incredible success with "Milk Does a Body Good" ad campaign. As a kid, I vividly remember the advertisements in print and on television. Steve stated, "The dairy industry tried for twenty years to convince you that milk is good for you. It's a lie, but they tried." [13] While Steve's talk wasn't focused on the dangers of cow dairy, I was amused that the genius shared his opinion regarding cow milk.

MEAT MONDAYS

So, what about me? I was asking my son to make all these food and drink changes, and I wasn't holding my own self accountable. *But why should I?* I didn't suffer from severe night coughing. I didn't have ear problems or any problem due to cow dairy. But after seeing the magical health results with Alec, I completely stopped drinking and eating cow dairy and followed in Alec's foot steps. *Thank you, Alec. You are my role model on this one!*

I didn't notice any changes with my body except one thing: congestion. Until I stopped consuming cow dairy, I hadn't ever noticed how much I actually did cough and blow my nose; mostly in the mornings. I do ever so often eat cow cheese (pizza or some yummy creamy dish) but, I pay for it the next morning by hacking up mucus and phlegm. Gross.

One day my lovely neighbor and I were having a conversation about nutrition, and I mentioned dairy alternatives. She suggested oat milk in addition.

"Oat milk?!" me.

"Yes, it naturally has a sweet taste to it. I think you'll like it," lovely neighbor.

(Me making a three year old soar face).

"Just give it a try," lovely neighbor.

At the time, I was having a playdate in her house, and I was cockroach cornered. I tried it. Not bad. I truly admire Betty. She is the picture of good health. Her dedication to being a vegan is admirable, but I don't have enough self-control. It's not in me. But through her encouragement and after watching a couple of documentaries she suggested (*Forks Over Knives* and *Cowspiracy*), I decided to test for one week as a vegetarian. I know it is trendy to do "Meatless Mondays", but I thought to give it at least a week. With the exception of a few hiccups, I did it!

After seeing how easy it was, I decided to try if I could go for one month. But I didn't want to be too extreme, and socially, I wanted to allow myself the freedom to order a dish with meat in a restaurant if I so desired. Basically, I have coined the phrase "Meat Mondays". I'm only eating meat about once a week and switch between using chocolate oat milk in my coffee and chocolate soy.

I started "Meat Monday" January 2016, and it's now one year later. I'm a vegetarian! The biggest changes I have noticed with my body are lighter periods and a little more energy. And I have been cow dairy free since 2015.

I know, I know…you still might be skeptical and not ready to wear on the vegetarian suit or sip on a soy milk latte. But maybe try a "Meatless Monday" and before you know it, you'll be a "Meat Monday" kind of person.

PETA (People for the Ethical Treatment of Animals) has an informative article posted on their website: http://www.peta.org/living/food/reasons-stop-drinking-milk/. But if you decide to keep drinking cow milk and live in the States, please at least buy organic milk.

Organic milk does not have rBGH - first developed by Monsanto; FYI, the genetically engineered hormone is banned in Europe and Canada! [14]

DOCTOR'S ORDERS

While Alec's intolerable coughing went away unfortunately, his ears did not get better. They were still clogged. Our HNO *Hals-Nasen-Ohren* (neck-nose-ears) doctor was very persistent and kept pushing us to get the surgery to insert small plastic ear tubes called myringotomy or tympanostomy.

We happened to be at our pediatrician's office for a regular check-up and mentioned the surgery in passing. She advised us to get a second opinion before going through with a surgery. So, off we went to another appointment at a HNO she recommended. We were shocked by the difference of opinion we received. After doing several tests, this was the new doctor's reply:

"I would not recommend a surgery for Alec since he is younger than two years-old. When general anesthesia is used - when they put the patient to sleep - this is too dangerous for such young children. If something is not life threatening, one should wait till at least two years of age." doctor.

"But what about his hearing? Won't this disable him or slow him down from learning?" me.

"His hearing is fine. It's not perfect, but it can wait until the summer. He reacts to your voice and is talking a little, correct?" doctor.

"Actually, he talks a lot in both German and English. One wouldn't think he has a problem at all," me.

Then I asked the doctor the question all parents want to know,

"Would you have the surgery on your own child?"

"Absolutely not. I would wait. We'll do check-ups every three to four months to see if it clears up and gets better," doctor.

It was an easy decision to make after that comment. And she was right. One of his ears did get better. But finally our doctor said that the other ear needed the surgery because Alec was at the age of important speech development. And so Alec had the surgery when he was two years and eight months old.

In the end, everything was ok but not free from added stress and drama. The surgery was planned for early morning, and Alec was to be discharged early afternoon. Jens had scheduled off work and everything was set. The day before the operation, we had to go in for a pre-surgery appointment at the hospital.

At the appointment, a doctor said that Alec (in addition to his ear operation) should have half of his tonsils removed. We were shocked because we had been going to HNO doctors for more than a year, and no one had ever said anything about Alec's tonsils needing to be removed; neither did our pediatrician.

It was less than 24 hours before the surgery, and the hospital needed our approval to go forward with the surgery right then and there at that moment. We had to make a decision on the spot. I wanted to do the surgery on a later date. The doctor explained it would be best to do everything at one time because Alec wouldn't have to go under again with anesthesia. But he would have to stay over night at the hospital. *Oh, God.* Jens and I both felt pressured. We were sitting in a hospital with a doctor surrounded by sterile pointy objects - so disorienting. I wanted to move the surgery date, but everything was already prepared and scheduled so, we signed the new operation papers.

The following day after the operation, the surgeon came out and gave us an update. During the surgery, she made the decision not to remove his tonsils. *Why?!* She explained that the doctor the day before had made a mistake. *What?!* She said that during the surgery she could get a better look at his tonsils. It was gut wrenching to know that Alec almost had half of his tonsils cut out. But we were so grateful that this unnecessary procedure did not happen.

A few days after, Alec had his checkup with his HNO. I told her what happened. This calm collected well-respected German doctor got mad. Her lips clamped together, face turned beat red, and her forehead got all scrunchy. She told me that unfortunately sometimes this occurs. She also informed me that she would be calling the hospital and asking them why they went against her orders. I would not want to be on the other end of that phone conversation.

There are several reasons for sharing Alec's ear story. First, it is a common surgery among kids; "about one million children each year have tubes placed in their ears". [15] Second, "the most common ages are from 1 to 3 years old" to have a this type of operation. [16] In some cases, it is best to have an immediate surgery even if the child is under two years old, but I would always get a second or third opinion in this situation. Third, our terrible experience and mix-up with the operation orders.

Here's *my* advice to parents. Always stick with your original doctor's orders. Your routine doctor(s) know your child best. If a hospital wants to change the operation orders, do not sign any papers until you speak with your child's doctor. I know the feeling of being pressured and gasping for oxygen while your frightened child sits in your lap, holding sweaty palms.

Chapter 4

Parenting and the Potty
Teaching your Child to Go

"She is still going poo in her pants." She is Gabi. And she is three and a half years old. But Gabi isn't the only one messing her pants. Since Alec is almost two, my ears perk up anytime someone mentions potty training. I begin to hear (and overhear) all the horrid stories from the moms on the playground and at the *kita*. Apparently there are lots and lots of three and four year olds refusing to pee and poo on the toilet.

I see plastic bags filled with wet, smooshed clothes hanging from strollers. The soils of potty training war. I also notice shoes in some bags. When a child pees their pants, it leaks into their underwear, shirt, pants, socks and down into the shoes. And if it's cold outside, all the extra layers including winter snow suits. There's a load or two!

I cringe and my stomach hurts to think about rinsing out all the peed and pooped-in clothes. I thought the days of shit were over. When

Alec was a baby, I never understood how it would literally ran up all the way to the back of his neck.

But I figure if I can master the art of getting my baby to sleep through the night and eating vegetables, surely I can tackle potty training. Or is it called toilet training? I have never called the big white mysterious bowl a potty or used the term for referring to use the bathroom so, I'll simply say "toilet training" from now on. Although, a lot of google searches will come up as "potty training" in the U.S.

So! How does one learn to toilet train their child? Reading! Education! Advice! Learning! Let's call it REAL. Let's get REAL. None of this *I'll just figure it out* business.

Because we had such great success with sleep schedules and training from Gary Ezzo, M.A. and Robert Bucknam, M.D., we also used their progressive toilet training methods in *On Becoming Toddler Wise: Parenting the First Childhood Eighteen to Thirty-six Months*. This book wasn't as profound as their first, but the section on toilet training is excellent.

About the time Alec is twenty-two months old, my mom asks me, "Why on earth haven't you toilet trained Alec yet?!" I clinched up and madly scurried around reading blogs. I was drawn to titles like 'toilet training over a weekend', 'toilet training in three days', and 'potty training in just one day'! I'm simply not interested in toilet/potty training methods that last six months to a year. No thank you. I stand by my philosophy of "hell for three days" and converge it into Alec's toilet training. I even searched 'potty training bootcamp' and got plenty of hits.

Many books and blogs talk about taking aside one weekend to completely focus on toilet training. I agreed with this weekend idea since Jens could join in the glorious mess. Misery loves company so, do it on a weekend!

WHO? WHO DECIDES TO BEGIN

The real reason I believe in these short scheme methods is because it works! After twelve hours of toilet training, our beloved son went pee in the toilet. And on the third day, he went poo in the toilet. I was so proud of Alec. And I was proud of my husband and I for teaching another priceless tool to our son.

But the maintenance lasts until your little darling can look at you with his beautiful eyes and say, "Mama, I have to go to the bathroom." Or in our case, "Peeeeee peeeee, Maaaamaaaaa!!!" I guess it depends on your definition of *toilet trained*. Yes, Alec went pee in the toilet the first day but only because we put him there. It was not his choice.

Lucky for parents if their toddler takes interest in toilet training at the age of two. This rarely occurs. For the rest of us, the initiative has to come from the parents. I overhear from other mothers that they are waiting to start until their child is ready. Ready for what? When is a child ever ready to do anything but eat and play? Yes, toddlers are curious about using the bathroom and might seem interested, but learning to use the toilet does not begin until the parents say *ok, it is time to start and no looking back*.

I'm telling you…parent to parent…looking straight into your eyes…most kids do not want to learn how to use the bathroom. Parents have to give "the right kind of guidance, encouragement, and sufficient opportunities to learn." [1]

WHEN & WHY TO START

Most American books and blogs I read explain that girls can start toilet training before the age of two and boys at two. The *Baby Whisperer* whispers to begin between eighteen months and two years when they have control of their sphincter muscles (basically having the capability to stop peeing midstream). [2] My mother concurs but adds that both genders can start even earlier. It is "estimated 50% of the world's children are toilet trained by the time they turn one". [3]

Alec started his hard core toilet training four days after his second birthday. I'm not sure if Alec was ready, but his parents were ready! But the whole learning process of toilet training started a couple of months before Alec turned two. Jens and I would bring him into the bathroom and let him watch how mama and papa did it. Then we would let Alec flush the toilet for fun.

Also, a week before starting, tell your child that you only have a week's worth of diapers (for daytime). Everyday count down to how many diapers are left to the big kid day of wearing no diapers! [4] Or have your child give them to a younger child who is still in diapers.

Alec is a copy and paste of Jens. Alec's appearance is identical to Jens' baby pictures. While Alec inherited his father's physical traits, he got his mom's loud, silly, goofy American traits. Since Alec has his father's strong physical genes, I decided to ask my mother-in-law if she remembers when she toilet trained Jens. She replied back instantly, "Around one and a half." What?! Wow! I told her everyone I knew in Germany starts toilet training around three years old, and the whole process is very relaxed and drawn out. It takes ages to learn to go to the bathroom. "Well, we didn't have diapers back then," she said, "I had to hand wash everything." Aha! There was her motivation!

I asked my mom if she used cloth diapering (in the seventies). "Of course," she said, "We were too poor to buy disposable diapers." My mom explained that diapers were not readily available and affordable like they are today. I reported my findings back to my mother-in-law, and she said there wasn't even an option to buy diapers in Germany. They were obsolete. "It was tough back then. People had no money for things like that," she said.

I felt bad that Alec had to wear diapers as long as he did. I thought about alternatives to disposable diapers - mainly cloth diapers. I hated the idea of him wrapped up in plastic every single second; especially when he was a newborn.

Also, all the diapers ending up in land fills is terrible for the planet. An average baby/toddler will use around six thousand disposable diapers [5]. I saw a cool thing where one major German car battery manufacture recycles diapers into batteries. They "wash" the diapers and melt down the diapers into plastic that is used to make the car battery. So, our babies wear the same material as a car battery. A car battery!

After all this to consider, I still used normal diapers on Alec. I'm all for alternatives; however, for me, I draw the line when it comes to poop. So, I was absolutely ready to get Alec out of diapers as soon as possible, and that's why I chose to start right at the age of two.

The longer parents wait to start toilet training the more problems will occur. For example, going poo in the toilet can be a challenge. A child might go pee but resist to go poo in the toilet. Parents have to put a diaper on for the chid to do their mess, and then take it off for disposal. A friend of mine had to cut holes in pull-up diapers for her daughter to learn to poo in the toilet. How frustrating and emotional it must be for a four year old child to have to still wear a pull-up diaper.

Also, studies have shown that later potty training can increase risk of urinary and bowel problems, for example, urinary tract infections and bladder control. [6]

Another reason to start earlier than later is because of a second child. I think this is partly what happened with our dear Gabi. A little baby brother came along when she was three years old. Mom and dad probably didn't have the time and energy to toilet train her with a newborn. And it's never a good idea to introduce a new routine to a toddler; especially with a new baby. I can't imagine the disruption and everyday occurrences from a baby while at the same time training a toddler to use the bathroom.

And, in the case of a second child, most are born two years after or later than the first. So, it's perfect timing to get toilet training out of the way before the second baby is born. And how do you toilet train your second, third or fourth child? Simple, they see their big brother or sister using the bathroom. Sure parents have to do some toilet training but one of the most difficult problems to solve in any new routine is uncovering the motivation of the child. And the motivation of a child is wanting to be like their older sibling(s). How many times have you witnessed or heard funny stories of children mirroring their older brother or sister?

HOW? PRODUCTS AND REWARDS

My husband and I thought it would be best for Alec to pee while sitting down. Apparently, this is a German thing. I never ever-ever once saw one of my ex-boyfriends sitting while peeing. Not to dwell on my love life, but I have dated many men from many different countries. I should be an honorary ambassador to the United Nations.

The "peeing while sitting" style for men is increasingly becoming popular due to the iPad. If you haven't already, please watch the movie *This Is 40*. There is a hilarious scene where the mom catches the dad escaping from fatherly duties while sitting on the toilet while playing a game on his iPad.

Also, we bought a portable toilet lid that laid on the bathroom floor for about a month, so Alec could be aware of yet another big plastic object which was to become a part of his life. Friends of ours had much success with simply training directly on the toilet without all the gadgets and gizmos. They taught their children how to climb up on their own. We used a special potty training lid for Alec, but he had no place to rest their feet. And he definitely needed help to park his cute little butt on the toilet. So, we had used a make shift plastic storage bin to rest his feet, but it wasn't cutting it.

On the thirteenth day of Alec learning how to use the bathroom, we bought him a toilet trainer lid with an attached step stool and handles. At first, Alec was scared and skeptical, but after a week, he built up his confidence to climb up and down the ladder. He loved it. I wish we had bought this brilliant step-ladder, lid toilet trainer from the very beginning! He used it for more than a year. I highly recommend it.

I'm not a fan of bribery, but in certain situations like toilet training, it's a must. Alec usually does what I tell him, but there are a few things he will not budge on. For example, going up and down the stairs in our apartment building.

The first three days of toilet training, we used fruit and vegetables as treats. Since Alec just turned two years old, he still had not tasted refined sugar and no desserts of any kind. So he was very pleased to receive bites of ripe banana, bell pepper, avocado, grapes and raisons. Dried mango work great too because of its high fiber content. All these foods/snacks help going poop a lot easier.

The day before starting to toilet train stay away from things that might cause constipation like cheese, rice, corn and too much meat. Select foods that are easy to digest and pass like avocados or beans.

It's the magical fruit! I have a great recipe for hummus in the appendix, too.

And no junk food as treats. This will lead to bad behavior and stressed out parents. There are plenty of healthy delicious options. I can't believe what I was reading in some books and websites to use as rewards: potato chips, candy, soda, cake and salted nuts - even in the book I suggest *On Becoming Toddler Wise*. [7]

Ok, we did use low salted nuts to make Alec thirsty so, he would crave more liquids to go pee. And when I sent Jens to go out and buy some peanuts, he returned with these:

Ur-Erdnüsse aus Bolivien (peanuts from Bolivia)

geröstet und gesalzen (roasted and salted)

Mix aus 3 erlesenen Erdnuss - Sorten (mix of three exquisite peanut varieties)

I had no idea that peanuts came in different sizes and tastes. One type was even harder to chew, but I grew accustom to liking it. But this is not the time to culinarize your child's palate.

Another reward for going to the bathroom are videos. But be aware that American videos will be saying *potty*. Alec had never heard the word potty once in his life and every single video used this word. And funny how the oh-so American "good job" phrase kept popping up in the videos. Coincidentally, I say this all the time. Jens thinks this is hilarious because it's such an American thing to say. I didn't realize this until he pointed this out. He's totally right.

I'm not sure why I didn't have more children's books about going to the bathroom for Alec. We had one Seasame Street book to read him while he sat on the toilet. And only one other book that showed a bathroom in which Alec would always say *mama poo poo* when we turned to that page. But he quickly understood why one uses the toilet.

On the second or third day, I heard Alec saying "poo poo." I sprinted into the living room and discovered him straddling his Playmobil airplane. He had taken the ceiling off the airplane and was pretending to go poo in the airplane's toilet. The toilet is about the size of a marshmallow.

The last type of reward to give your toddlers are toys. Every book and blog suggests The Dollar Store or in our case, The Euro Store. But I was completely over small, cheap toys. Alec had just received twenty-four of them from his Christmas advent calendar. Surely, Jens didn't want Alec to have a present for each day, but I was wrong.

"Of course," Jens.

"But every day?" me.

"Yes," Jens.

"Really? Every day for twenty-four days you want him to get a gift?" me.

"Yes," Jens.

End of discussion. So, I filled twenty-four little Christmas stockings with small books, balloons, toy animals, cars and anything else that would fit into a jean pocket size stocking. One thing I have definitely learned from the Germans is you don't mess around with their Christmas traditions.

HOW CONTINUED: TRAINING DAY BY DAY

Listed below are Alec's first ten days of pee and poo occurrences. As a parent unfamiliar to toilet training, I know this is information overload. But I wish that I had something like this when we were teaching Alec.

We started on a Thursday during Christmas/New Year holiday. I thought four days of practice before he returned to *kita* from the holiday break would be sufficient.

Day 1: Since Alec was naked from the waist down, he peed all over the floor and pooped twice. It was a mess. But we didn't yell or discipline him. We kept repeating that he must tell mama and papa when he has to go to the bathroom. And we would take the poop in a gazillion layers of paper towels to the toilet and plop it in with Alec. We told him that this is where the poo poo goes, and he should only go poo poo in the toilet. We let him flush the toilet, and he would say, "Poo poo gone! Bye bye!"

By early afternoon, Alec would tell us right away if he peed or pooped on the floor. He would say, *nass* (wet). It would be a long time till he was able to tell us before hand if he had to use the bathroom. But him telling us that he used the bathroom - even on the floor - was a good sign. It was a small step in the learning process.

12 hours into toilet training at 6:00pm, Alec went pee in the toilet. Wahoo! It worked! It was a long day, and it was getting close to his bed time. I was beginning to think that it wasn't going to happen. But he did it, and we were so happy!

But let me explain that Alec only went pee on the toilet because we put him there. He did not say he had to go pee. Parents have to become familiar with their child's routine. We finally realized this on the third day of toilet training. I couldn't grasp how Alec was suppose to learn to go on the toilet if he couldn't tell us when he had to go. I re-read some websites (no skimming) and learned that a two year old toddler in training can go pee every 45 minutes to an hour.

I wish I had known this before. What we were doing was waiting for Alec to have to go pee and then taking him to the bathroom. We were looking for signs that he needed to go to the bathroom. We were also waiting for Alec to actually say he had to go pee. We asked hundreds of times if he had to go pee or poo. Every time we got a "*nein*" (no) and then a couple of minutes later, he would pee or poop on the floor. So, learn from our mistake and don't wait till your child says, "I have to go pee pee," because your little darling is not going to say it. Simply park their cute lil' butt on the toilet every fort-five minutes to an hour. We set the oven timer and let Alec push the button off. Then a pit stop at the bathroom.

Day 2: Alec peed three times in the toilet! Hooray! But he pooped twice again on the floor. One of the times that Alec peed on the toilet is because I saw him grab his penis while playing. I immediately snatched him and raced to the toilet. He went! I thought that him grabbing his penis would be a future signal to tell me when he had to go pee. Nope. Never happened again.

Day 3: In the morning, Alec peed twice in the toilet. And he went from being totally nude from the waist down to now wearing underwear! But I thought Alec would have progressed more. Please don't judge me, but after 2 1/2 days of only doing toilet training, I was becoming a little impatient. During his nap, I re-read some toilet training blogs.

So I read that parents should put their little one on the toilet every 45 minutes to an hour. We stuck by that tip. And that afternoon, Alec went pee and poo on the toilet! Delightful! I think we were so pleased that I didn't keep track of the next time Alec would have to go pee. Sure enough, one hour and five minutes later, Alec was sitting in my lap while I was reading a book to him, and he peed on me.

Day 4: Alec peed five times in the toilet. Good job, son! However, in the morning, he pooped twice in his underwear. Argh! I thought that he needed some new treats for motivation so, I ventured out to the grocery store and bought *dinkelkeks* (baby/toddler cookies) for the first time. I squinted my eyes for half an hour looking at all the different ingredients and counting the sugars. I settled on two types that are both bio. One of them is for babies from eight months old, sweetened with rice syrup and banana, and it only had five ingredients. The other one is from fifteen months old, sweetened with agave, honey, and ten other ingredients. Alec loved these; a little too much. Every time he sits on the toilet, he points upwards and says, "Cookie, two cookies." Then I negotiate it down to one cookie or a few raisins. Of course, distracting him by showing a music video of "The Wheels on the Bus" always works, too. This is by far his favorite reward.

Day 5: Alec peed twice before *kita* and once after. He pooped twice in the toilet (at home). Wahoo! This was Alec's first day back at *kita* from the Christmas/New Year break. And the *kita* did not share in our enthusiasm in toilet training Alec (more on that later).

Day 6: Alec peed 3 times and pooped once. He stayed home from *kita* on this day as I was a more than annoyed with the *kita's* attitude toward helping Alec use the bathroom.

But luckily we got invited to a three year olds birthday party and got out of the house that afternoon. I went back and forth trying to decide if I should bring our big blue chunk of plastic toilet training lid. I knew in my gut that Alec would not go to the bathroom. What little kid wants to get dragged away from a party to use the toilet? So, I put a pull-up diaper on him and shoved the unsightly toilet training lid into a plastic bag. We might not be using it at the party, but I was determined for Alec to see that this not so chic accessory would be coming with us. By the way, he didn't use it. Sigh.

Today, we also started with one of those toilet training sticker charts. I wish I began this sooner. I never thought Alec would respond with such excitement and pleasure as much as food given as a reward for using the bathroom. I found a ton of print-outs on Pinterest, but Alec and I ended up making one together.

Alec's interest in the sticker charts lasted for two weeks. But he still loved the stickers so, he decorated his favorite car with them when he used the toilet. That car goes every where with him, but I don't allow it out of the house or in his bed at night. No toys in the bed while sleeping.

Day 7: Alec peed twice and pooped once. We had another playdate in the afternoon so, all the action was happening in his pull-up diaper. But twice he told me he had to go poo poo. The blue lid fit on my friend's toilet, and Alec happily sat on it. Nothing happened, but it was the first time using the lid outside our home. Lots of kisses for Alec and two grapes!

Day 8: Alec peed 5 times and pooped 3 times. Terrific!

Day 9: Alec peed 8 times.

Day 10: Alec peed 6 times and pooped 3 times. Jens and I are extremely pleased with our young gentleman.

RUMBLE AT THE KITA

To my surprise, I got more than a bit of backlash from our *kita* about toilet training Alec too early. I knew I might receive some hesitation considering most of the kids in our *kita* did not start training until they were at least three-years-old.

The day we returned to the *kita* after the holiday break (this would be Alec's fifth day of training), I handed the head caretaker a letter Jens had wrote in German stating that Alec had begun toilet training and explained the progress he had made. We asked that the *kita* continue to help Alec like any other developmental step. We also said that Alec will wear pull-up diapers so, they won't have to clean up any messes, but requested that they take him to the bathroom every hour when possible.

Immediately the caretaker responded saying that there are too many children, and they could not help with his toilet training. I gave her a look. She quickly responded, "Well, of course we can help. We take some children to the toilets after breakfast and lunch. We'll take Alec, too."

When I returned at 2pm to pick up Alec, I asked if he used the toilet.

"No, he was very scared," said the caregiver.

Well, of course he's scared I thought.

"Ok, maybe I can help. Since Alec starts *kita* at 9am, we could come at 8:45am. Then I can help him get use to the toilet here," me.

"No, you shouldn't do this. We have to do it. He has to learn that we will help him," caretaker.

The next day I picked up Alec, I asked the same question.

"Did Alec use the toilet?" me.

"No, he was scared again," caretaker.

"Ummm…ok. Did he even sit on the toilet?" me.

"I don't know. It was a very busy day," caretaker.

I could tell she was annoyed with me. I know our *kita* has a lot of work and has deal with many parents. I always go out of my way to keep it short and simple when I drop off and pick up Alec. I rarely ask the caretakers about him. I say hello, good-bye and thank you.

So, on the third day, I didn't ask if he went pee or poo. I decided to use action instead of words. Whenever I picked up Alec from the *kita*, I would take him to the toddler toilettes. I didn't ask anyone. I didn't get anyone's permission. I just did it.

The first couple of times we just sat in front of the small toilets and spoke about using them at the *kita*. After a few days, I put Alec on the toilet and held onto him. Then after one week, Alec did it! I'm not sure why he was so reluctant, but we took our time and sure enough he went pee. For the first few weeks, I always had some sort of treat for him in the stroller if he went to the bathroom, for example, a small piece of banana bread.

Being ever so annoyed with our *kita* - which I usually applaud, I set out to find other moms to see if they were having similar difficulties with the staff. I remembered one mom saying her son showed interest in using the toilet a few months before. The next day I ran into her, and she had time for a quick chat. Her son is two weeks younger than Alec.

"Has Marc started toilet training yet?" me.

"He already uses the bathroom," Gloria.

"What?! Really?!" (this is usually how all my parenting responses begin).

"Yeah, he goes right on the toilet. He loves it. He always asks to go," Gloria.

"Wait. He tells you when he has to go pee or poo?" me.

"Yes. Every time. And he gets so excited because I will give him one raison. Can you believe it? One raison. One raison!" Gloria.

I didn't say one word about all the different kinds of rewards I have for Alec and the amounts. Alec would laugh in my face if I gave him one raison. And actually the same afternoon I gave Alec one raison for going pee pee to see his reaction. He started demanding two raisons. I gave him two more. Then another two. This lasted until he received eight raisons and one *dinkelkeks* shaped as a cat.

"So, I don't get it. I thought I saw Marc wearing a diaper today at the *kita* this morning?" me.

"Oh, at the *kita*, he still wears diapers and at home underwear. He is always asking to wear his underwear. Sometimes we have to tell him no when we go over to someone's house. We're afraid he might have an accident. But at home he wears underwear," Gloria.

"Why haven't you spoken to the *kita*?" me.

"We have," she said with an agitated look, "They said he should start with toilet training this summer."

"This summer?! That's in another six months!" me.

"Yes, well, you know how it is here," Gloria.

"No, I don't know how it is here," me.

Gloria is studying to be a child caretaker. She is in her fifth year at a university in Hamburg. She explained - with a lot of eye rolling - that in her classes they are taught to let the child decide when it is time for them to learn how to use the toilet. Some don't start till they are five years old. Over the next few years I would discover that German children, at least in Hamburg, start very late with toilet training.

I never envisioned Alec wearing pull-ups. Let's all tell the truth. It's a diaper. Unfortunately, Alec had to wear them at the *kita* but underwear at home like Marc. Let me tell you, nothing...nothing is cuter than your toddler running around in underwear. I bought Alec days-of-the week underwear. Any time I can create more opportunities to learn, I do it; however, there is a down side with this type of underwear. It might cause some frantic freak-outs.

Alec was wearing his Wednesday's, and I was suppose to have a doctor appointment on Tuesday. In reality, it was Tuesday morning. Only I panicked when I saw him walking down our hallway with his Wednesday underwear on. And for a short moment, I thought it was Wednesday, and I had missed my appointment.

Learn from me, don't buy your little one days of the week

underwear. Just be "normal" and let your child choose which underwear they want at the store for their first time.

Also, when it comes to a toddler training in underwear, here's a tip: put a panty liner in them. They soak up about half the pee so, clean up is easier. And enough runs down their leg to know they had an accident. That's the point with toilet training. You want your child to know that they are wet or dirty. This makes them feel uncomfortable and in return, hopefully they will want to stay dry and clean. With pull-ups, they will never feel wet and uncomfortable. And that's exactly the purpose of a diaper; therefore, a pull-up is still a diaper.

Day 33: A huge break through. Alec finally tells us when he has to go to the bathroom. Then, by himself, he runs to the bathroom, climbs up his ladder, and sits on the toilet. We still have to help him with his pants and underwear.

About a week earlier, I repeatedly told Alec that he can go *all by himself.* I started to use this phrase a lot around the house.

"Alec, carry your plate to the dining room. All by yourself."

"Alec, put your teddy bear in the bed. You can do it. All by yourself."

"Look at Alec! He is doing it all by himself."

"Alec, can you put your dirty clothes in the laundry basket? Good! Alec did it all by himself."

"Alec, you can go the bathroom all by yourself. You don't have to tell mama or papa. You can just go. All by yourself."

"Show mama how you can go to the bathroom all by yourself."

He soon began to add, "Alec *macht,*" (makes) when doing things by himself.

NAP AND NIGHT TIME DRYNESS

Of course if you live in France or send your child to a French school, you don't have to worry about toilet training. The school will teach them. No questions, no glares, no judgement. Public and private schools toilet train. It is part of the school's curriculum. *Comment aimez-vous les pommes?* (How do you like those apples?)

When Alec was two years and nine months old, he started at the International French School (Lycée Antoine de Saint Exupéry) in the petite section. His teachers were pleased that he was already toilet trained, and they were annoyed with the German children that were not.

And I was so grateful for the teachers the first day! Alec had achieved naptime dryness! His daycare teachers simply took all the children to the toilet before their nap and immediately after. The nap was one and a half hours. On the weekends, I followed the caregivers example, and it has worked every single time.

This also could have easily been done sooner in Alec's German *kita* but *nein*! When it comes to toilet training, if you do not have the support of your daycare it will be an unpleasant, drawn out, cumbersome process. As much as I hate to admit this, it might make more sense not to start toilet training until the daycare says it's time to start. It makes my blood boil to think of all the children in Germany that are capable of using the toilet by themselves, but the daycare is not supportive. In the U.S. and France, parents do not run into this problem as much - if at all.

Achieving night time dryness is trickier because there is a huge range of when your little one will stay dry all through the night - on average it happens around 33 months. [8] However, one's interpretation of night time dryness has different meanings. Let me share our story.

We were on a family vacation in Switzerland when Alec was three years and three months old. We shared an apartment with another family that we knew well. They have a son with only a two months age difference with Alec. Although they live far apart, the boys have been growing up together. We all see each other two or three times a year.

A constant topic of conversation during the vacation was toilet training and making sure the boys didn't have any accidents. Being that both our boys are only children, they hadn't witnessed how other children were going to the bathroom at home. In addition, what a big deal other parents were making about staying dry.

In a few days, they both started acting out - in a positive way - regarding going to the bathroom. For example, the other little boy was still wearing diapers during his nap and other special times like when he went to ski school. He started to scream and cry when his parents would put a diaper on him. With Alec, he would flat out refuse a diaper at bed time. Jens and I were shocked. We didn't know what to do. We couldn't risk Alec wetting the bed. We promised Alec that when we returned to Hamburg he didn't have to wear a diaper at night anymore. Through some negotiation and tears, Alec agreed.

As promised, we didn't put a diaper on Alec at bed time. He was so proud of himself. We were too until Alec would wet the bed at all hours of the night. For months, I was washing sheets almost every day. But Alec continuously refused a diaper in the evening.

Insanity struck and I posted in an expat mother Facebook group searching for solutions to bedwetting. There was a lot of activity on it.

Here's my Facebook post, and the following are the comments I received which were helpful and reassuring:

"Night time bed wetting blues. Help! So sick of doing laundry. Our son did really well with potty training - two years old! And for naps, no diaper for a long time. He is three and a half but still wets the bed at night... Maybe 50% of the time. I learned a really great trick from a German mom that has worked really well but still some accidents; around 11pm before my husband goes to bed, he picks him up and puts him on the toilet. He goes straight back to bed-no sleep problem. Any other ideas out there? I'm not pushing our son but just wondering if I could be missing any fantastic, life breaking tip. TIA"
~ Marlane Wingo

Facebook Comments:

If his body isn't ready, you can't force it (unfortunately).
Maybe it's easier if you put a potty next to his bed?!
* (Marlane Wingo) My response = He hates wearing a diaper - refuses. But after his 11pm pee, we put a diaper on him, and he goes back to sleep immediately.

It took our daughter some time to get up on her own to the toilet, and the "oh! Have to pee in the middle of the night!" awareness was the last thing for us to be 100%. (A couple months after she turned 4). So we did night time pull-up thingers during that transition which seemed to work fine, and I think at one point she declared she didn't need them anymore and didn't.

I hear you the washing is mad. What's helped a lot here is restricting liquids before bed time to a shot glass of milk or water, making going to the toilet part of the bedtime routine, sleeping without bottoms on and also layers of sheets and waterproof sheet to whip the covers off quicker in the night when it does happen. But we still have accidents quite often especially when she's really tired. Heard that is normal for a lot of years yet though. Need a washing fairy or some sun to dry all the sheets... Good luck!

It worked with my son.......(Enutrain - electrotherapy with dampness sensor)

I also recommend this (Enutrain) and can be prescribed by your Kinderarzt (pediatrician). Ours was reluctant before the boys were 7 unless the child was distraught. We started using from 6 and has worked well after the first month of mishaps. We tried training before but when your child is put on the toilet asleep or distraught disorientated etc. I believe your wish is over riding the child's physical readiness.

We did pull ups which we called nighttime pants, NEVER nappies. I also said that when it's dry 5 times in a row, he can go without. But we did that from the start so not sure it would work in your situation. Good luck!

We also restrict fluids after 5:30/6pm and if she's drunk a lot we usually take her to the loo as soon as we hear her stir because inevitably she wets the bed at that time (I think she's just in too deep a sleep to wake up at that point, later in the night is no problem). Like the other mom, we layer the bed so it's quicker to change the sheets in the night. But another tip I have is telling/retelling that when she dreams of water or going to the toilet it usually means she needs to wee. I also find its much worse when she's growing or going through a developmental phase ...

Oh I know the case...
You won't like it but I think that 11pm is too early to take him to the toilet. Then you leave him with approximately 8h of holding. I have noticed that if you take the child at night to the toilet exactly 4 to 5-5 hours after he went to bed he won't have an accident. So if he goes to bed at around 8pm you should wake him up at around 12:30am and you won't have any bedsheets to wash the next day. If you know that he has drunk a lot of liquids before going to bed then take him to the

toilet max 4 hours after going to bed. I know it's a pain to get up in the midnight to take him to the toilet but that's the way it works. The night control is a milestone that can happen from one day to the other suddenly, it's as if their brain clicks and sends the right signal at the right time. And this happens one nice night.

We have the same issue with our four year old. He needs to pee once a night but he simply does not wake up. He dislikes his nappies but absolutely, for reasons unknown, hates pull-ups and refuses to wear them. I have taken the view that at some point his body will learn not to have to pee at all during the night and that we simply wait with taking off the diaper until it he wakes up with a dry one in the morning. Now I am a bit concerned that I expect waaayy too much and that by continuing that way, he will still be in diapers when he is going to school ... ???
* Another mom's response = Haha it'll happen eventually. Max has been going to toilet in the night since he was 2 1/2 but then he's super lousy at other things.
* Original mom's response = Well, basically, what I am asking is whether it is at all realistic for small kids to not have to pee at all at night. We tried to take him to the toilet at night but he goes absolutely berserk when we do, and starts screaming and shouting to let him sleep. I think he is so deeply asleep that he does not understand what is happening (i.e. us trying to take him to the toilet) yet half-awake enough to put on an impressive fight. We thus have given up on that, because no one really goes back to sleep for a while after that ...

All I have to add is that "accidents" are normal and can happen until your child is 12. I know because we've been to several specialists with our son. Even a longer stay at a hospital. So patience really is the key. I know it's hard.

* (Marlane Wingo) My response to everyone in the thread = Thanks guys!!!! Really appreciate it. Reassuring to know that Alec is normal and we are doing our best.

It took our daughter a long time too, my husband use to carry her to the toilet at 11pm as well. Then he got sick, but I couldn't carry her, so I woke her up fully (hard work!) and she went to the toilet herself. 2 weeks of this and she didn't wet the bed anymore. Has not had an accident in 3 months.

It's driven by hormones. Latest age 7 there is a hormone stopping pee production during night hours. There is nothing your lil' one can do to stop that consciously.

My son didn't want to wear diapers at night anymore either and we had some annoying wet nights. But then we sold him on "nighttime underpants" with the pull ups. It took some convincing but now it's the routine and he doesn't think to go to sleep without them.

My son was still wearing night diapers at 4, until a PD here told us to stop. We did. I woke him about twice at night and restrict his water intake prior to sleep. He is 6 now and maybe has wetted the bed less than 5x since. But it is really up to individual. My nephew at 11, still wet his bed at times regardless of the many effort by my sister-in-law.

Wow very young. Our son only came out of pull ups after 6th birthday due to obvious emotional needs. Our *Kinderarzt* felt very strongly this was normal for 50% boys and after tests agreed to the Enutrain paid by *Krankenkasse* (health insurance). In September he turns 7 and he is *halbtrocken* (medium-dry)..i.e. no liquids after 18.00, we wake him at 23.00 for the toilet and then dry through the night. With this method he is 98% successful but still would sleep through a wet bed...so as my *Artz* (doctor) said do not compare boys and girls and unless there is a hormonal issue they will be dry when their bodies are ready. Daytime and Nighttime dryness are not in sync..for us toilet training was fast and easy from 3...the rest is ongoing. Also the *Artz* was unhappy to intervene before he was 7 unless he was distressed.

If it helps, my daughter (5 years old) still wets her bed if she's in deep sleep. It's not very often but it does happen. Alec is still so little....I don't think you are missing anything. [9]

MAKING A PLAN

So, after reading all the comments and reassessing everything, Jens and I decided to stick with the German mom's suggestion of Jens putting Alec on the toilet but at 10pm. Then Jens puts him back to bed with a pull up diaper. Alec is barely awake and doesn't mind the diaper at all. In the morning, Alec goes straight to the bathroom, removes the diaper and goes to the toilet. Alec is now three years and eight months and wakes up fifty percent of the time dry. No tears. No fuss. No laundry.

We allow Alec to drink as much water as he likes in the evening. For some reason, I can not forcefully take away his right to drink water. If your child doesn't drink that much liquids in the evening, you might not have to put them on the toilet until 11pm.

Reporting back at 4 years of age. Alec still goes to bed wearing underwear, and Jens puts him on the toilet for him to pee at 10pm. Then he puts on the pull-up diaper. About seventy-five percent of the time, Alec wakes up dry. And when he does wake up dry, we praise him like a Sunday choir.

One more tip - especially for parents with only one child or the first child - if your child is being stubborn or having problems in learning any step of the process of going to the bathroom, let them watch their best friend do it. For example, if your child refuses to wash their hands after going to the toilet. Or doesn't want to pull up and down their underwear. Or a boy that does not want to hold his penis while peeing outside on a tree. Or whatever! A child watching their best buddy doing something correctly, and then receiving a lot of praise is enormous motivation.

Parents worldwide share a cultural trait regarding children using the bathroom. When everyone is dressed and ready to walk out the door, there is always one quiet peep, "I have to go pee pee."

Chapter 5

Parenting and the Other
Teaching your Child to live in a Multicultural World

ALL ROADS LEAD TO PARIS

When traveling in France, one has to go through Paris. Even if you are south of Paris and want to go further south, the network of highways and railroads will bring passengers to Paris, spin them around, and send them back south. The same is true in life. One has to go through Paris. It is the connection for fashion, romance and all the other clichés that everyone loves to indulge in. Tragically, I have discovered that I am Paris-less.

- I don't have a decent wardrobe - my style is a hodgepodge of the Spice Girls' looks.
- I don't fuss about perfume - mine costs less than twenty bucks a bottle.
- I'm not thin - I'm more of a seasonal fat wearer.
- I don't smoke - I actually want to start an anti-smoking

campaign in Hamburg.

- I can't wear bright, flirty, red lipstick; even the expensive high-pigment kind - I look like a washed-up, tired, old prostitute.

Paris also has France's top three universities and MBA programs. If you want your little darling to have the option someday of being in Airbus management or working in the European Parliament, it wouldn't be a bad idea for them to attend one of these.

In preparation for Alec to be the Airbus CEO or President of the EU Council, we stuck to our original plan of moving to Lokstedt for him to go to the International French School (Lycée Antoine de Saint Exupéry). He began with their daycare and later grade school.

On top of barely knowing any French, the bigger problem looming was choosing our first-day-of-school outfits for mom and son. I may come from the land where pajama jeans thrive, but I was determined not to make a complete *imbécile* of myself.

A couple of days before Lycée started, I slothed through my closet for a good half hour. In mommy time, this is equivalent to three hours. I noticed a ton of navy blue and vintage clothes; perhaps I do dawn a speck of French fashion. I settled on a chic, classic trench coat that would cover up my ill-fitting pants. I already put on my winter weight. I had some cool oxford shoes that would hopefully distract from everything else going wrong with my outfit.

For Alec, it took me a total of two minutes to select his clothes. For a little Bavarian flare, I picked out a gingham blue and white dress shirt, khaki pants and 'Wednesday' underwear for Alec. I'm not certain why the school begins in the middle of the week but whatever; they're French. I'm sure it was for some efficient reason.

On the Tuesday evening before the first day of French daycare,

Alec got sick. Terribly sick. It was our very first car ride in our very brand new car. My child's lovely vomit went everywhere in the car and continued into our very new apartment. We didn't make it to the first day. Luckily, he felt better, and I only had to switch the Wednesday underwear to the Thursday.

THE morning, I felt panicky and self-conscious about my outfit, and I required a confidence booster. I temporarily forgot my feminist views and spent forty-five minutes fixing my hair. I straightened it to get that freakishly-long, time consuming, polished look. For some unknown reason, it was taking me just as long to straighten it even though my hairdresser chopped-off half my hair earlier that summer.

I got "The Marlane" hairstyle. It's basically the opposite of "The Rachel". I have had the same haircut since I was two years old, and I was thirty-six years overdue for a new one. Also, those wretched gray hairs were sneaking in, too. I discovered a great trick for those pesky antenna grays is by covering them up with mascara: cheap, normal, run-of-the-mill mascara. I concluded to accept the every-day gray hairs but thought short gray hairs are better than long ones.

I can't pull off bobs so, I thought why not keep the length in the front and cut it short in the back? I came up with an A-Line/angled bob - similar to Victoria Beckham's style back in 2008; except mine is extremely long in the front. With "The Marlane", I can still pull my hair back into a ponytail.

A friend stated to me, "Well, that certainly isn't a mom-haircut." Initially, it wasn't my goal to have a non-mom haircut, but perhaps it's taking me further away from being Paris-less. And the radical contrast matches with my Dr. Jekyll and Mr. Hyde abnormal behavior. I have self-diagnosed myself as having a Borderline Personality Disorder.

I will eat a cucumber and tomato salad for lunch, followed up with a chocolate bar. I'll read a trashy novel, then a six-hundred-page book about Middle Eastern history. I'll go on a gluten-free diet for three solid weeks and then eat Mexican food every single day for a month. My idea of a gluten-free diet consists mostly of eating gluten free brownies, rice waffles and corn chips - not a typical meal for a Parisian.

SETTLING INTO OUR FRENCH VILLAGE

Feeling scared as heck for Alec's first drop-off and pick-up at French daycare, I took a two-week intensive French course. This was to learn the French language, not to learn how to dress or act like a Parisian woman; although, if a *Volkshochschule* (adult education center) offered a class on how to be a Parisian, I would be sitting center in the front row. On top of being Paris-less, my French is *horrible* and *terrible*. The word horrible and terrible is the same in French and English. I *adore* when this occurs.

My fear of not even being able to say *bonjour* properly or a quick introduction terrified me. Until this French class, I have been mispronouncing Elle magazine as "ehlay" and the word croissant by saying it with a hard "T" at the end.

Seriously, here's the best tip to know about French: leave off the last letter. Drop it. It seems like an easy thing to comprehend, but for my peanut size brain, it's a difficult concept to grasp. I continue to work on it every day.

I was the absolute worst student in my French class. For some reason, I don't mind butchering the German language because German does sound like one is hacking away on a meat bone, but to mutilate the French language is criminal. Mine is a bloodbath. And I drove the teacher crazy by whispering when called upon. She looked like an ostrich ducking her head up and down when saying, "What did you say? Can you repeat that? Can you speak a little louder, please?" She would ask, in English, for her dear American student that was only required to take one year of a foreign language in the good ol' public school system back in the States

The first day at Lycée went smoothly. I shall not mention the second or the third day. Alec had no tears, and I was able to communicate sufficiently in German and a bit of French. I strained to hear another person speaking English. Nope. I barely heard German. A few weeks into Lycée, I did chase down a mom in Alec's class that spoke English and befriended her; whether she liked it or not.

Lycée is an ethnic enclave: a 'Francetown' - as in Chinatown; however, there are no plastic-lucky gold cats, no dragon medicine balls, no buddha belly statues, no uncountable amount of red new year decorations, and no Peking ducks hanging by a noose. Instead, in Francetown, there are French dads pimped out with cuff links, carrot & celery leek soup served for lunch, a gazillion *bonjours* exchanged, and children with hyphenated names. I found out rather quickly one is supposed to say both names. The only uber-French stereotype that stands out are the Breton striped shirts that both kids and adults wear; also, an exuberant amount of *voilàs*. Most of the students have one French parent, they are from a French speaking country, or they come from a former French colony. This tiny section of Hamburg, with a radius less than a quarter of a kilometer is a French enclave.

We seemed to be one of the few Airbus families in Alec's class. I was counting on the Airbus connection to make friends. I thought surely there would be more especially since many French people are working at Airbus in Hamburg.

Only after three weeks at Lycée, Alec started speaking some

French. I nearly blacked out. Good thing we were playing in a sand box to break my fall.

"What did you do today at French school?" I asked.

"Cars," Alec said.

"Did you do anything else besides play with cars?" I asked.

"Ramps. Cars and ramps. Cars go ramps," Alec said.

"Oh, ok. The cars went up and down the ramps. Did you speak any French today? Ummm...*Bonjour? Merci?*" I asked.

"*Bonjour! Comment ça va?*" Alec replied.

This is when I was momentarily feeling light-headed seeing staticky gray and white dots.

"*Bonjour?!* Oh my god!!" I exclaimed.

"No, mama!!! *Bonjour!!! Comment ça va!!!*" Alec shouted.

"Oh, yes! I'm so sorry! I forgot to say, *comment ça va,*" I remarked.

On the weekend, he began saying *oui* and *merci*. That Sunday, I was getting ready to go for a run - ok, a slow jog - and as I was closing the door to leave, I heard a mouse peep, *"Au revoir."*

I'm loving the class activities. The next week his teacher showed us a bucket of potatoes the kids had dug up. The students from the previous year planted them. I wondered if Alec knew how to say potato in French. I wrestled with asking him. Am I expecting too much? Am I a Tiger Mom? Will he fall behind in class? He wasn't even three years old at the time.

"Alec, how do you say potato in French?" I asked wincing.

"*La pomme,*" without missing a beat.

Sunbeams and rainbows shot out of me. Good grief, it's working! My child speaks English and German and now French! I wondered when he should begin with Spanish and Japanese. Or should he learn

Chinese instead of Japanese?

The next day, I boasted to a small group of Lycée moms that Alec had said *la pomme*. My soon-to-be best mom French friend pulled me aside and quietly pointed out…*la pomme* means apple.

Ok, so 'potato' is *la pomme de terre,* but his language progress was blowing my little, naive, American mind. By the fourth week, I was teaching him a few colors and to count to six. At the moment, I couldn't remember: seven, eight, nine, ten.

It took some time to settle into a rhythm at Lycée and for Alec to feel comfortable. Meeting new friends and seeing familiar faces is always comforting - for mama, too. I met some wonderful parents after repeatedly pounding them with, "Hello! *Bonjour!*" I can't bring myself to only saying *bonjour*. It sounds so ridiculous coming out of my mouth. And I feel the need to translate everything I say in French to English or my mangled German.

But to my credit, during the first month, I didn't wear any black, stretchy, work-out pants with running shoes for the drop offs and pick-ups. But soon enough, I squeezed my legs into the sausage casing, and a mom declared, "You're so sporty!" Uh, oh. Sporty Spice had been unveiled.

THE LOUD AMERICAN

In Hamburg, I'm known as the loud American. I never regarded myself as loud. Ever. That is until I landed in Germany. I might not be a flag waving American, but I am loud. I'm also overly friendly. Again, I never noticed until living in Germany. With any new parent at Alec's *kita* and at Lycée, I would stick my hand out if they wanted to shake it or not. I'm the in-your-face welcome-wagon American. I even know a few of the DHL (similar to UPS) guys in our neighborhood by name. My favorite is Abdul.

Most of my friends in Hamburg tell me that hardly any parents speak to each other while dropping off and picking up their children at the *kita*: little eye-contact, very few '*guten morgen*' (good morning). I guess Americans - excuse me, North Americans - have nailed the cheerful 'hello' even when our lives are withering away in horse shit.

Even the French exchange a plethora of *bonjours*. By greeting one another with hellos, we acknowledge the other person's humanity. [1] This goes for children, too. I continually tell Alec to exchange hello, in the appropriate language with his friends and adults.

After a few cheerful hellos to one particular mom, I grasped that she spoke English and decided to take it to the next level. At the right moment, I stuck out my hand and introduced myself. Turns out, she's incredibly sweet! I invited her over for a playdate. Good times! The next playdate, she said, "Marlane, I want to tell you something." She explained how touched she was that I took the initiative and spoke to her. She said not one parent at the daycare had ever spoken to her. And she and her son had never been invited to anyone's home. I didn't know what to say. I was shocked and humbled by her comment. We both gained so much; not only our friendship but our sons' friendship. They quickly became best buddies.

OH LÀ LÀ!

Six months later, here is Alec's language progress report:

His ability to switch between English and German is effortless. And when Jens speaks in German, Alec turns to me and translates it to English - without me asking. *Uh, thanks*. Also, Alec speaks about 50% English and 50% German. And he doesn't just play in German any more. Whenever I am in the same room, he talks to himself in English or French while playing. But he still speaks German with his friends unless at playdates with English speaking friends. As for his French, his teachers say that he understands everything. Of course his speech is limited, but they are extremely pleased with his level given that French is not spoken in our home.

Here is Marlane's language progress report:

Zilch. A big fat zero. Nothing. I have not learned any French; therefore, I have not been able to help Alec progress with his French. The guilt is with me every day as I scribble it on my list of things-to-do but somehow it never seems to get done. I checked-out many library books in French for Alec. But I rarely reached for them at story time because I can't pronounce most of the vowel combinations.

I did stick a few post-it-notes around the house for Alec (and me):

1. How do you say that in French? *Qu'est-ce qu c'est en français?* (This note is in several places in our house to remind me to ask him.)

2. Whose turn is it? *C'est à qui?* It is mine. *C'est à moi.* (These are posted on his game and puzzle shelf.)

After I asked him a few *Qu'est-ce qu c'est ___ en français?* (How do you say ___ in French?), he answered correctly and then started rattling off French like his name was Jean-Jacques. I ran to the kitchen and exclaimed to Jens, "You gotta get in here! Alec is speaking French! I don't understand anything he is saying, but he's speaking French!" I tried to keep him speaking with my limited vocabulary. I quickly thought to play his favorite game - traffic sign dominos. I knew I could use my new found question *C'est à qui?* (Whose turn is it?) He didn't want to play it so, instead we ran around playing police car chase. We took turns playing the police car so, I was able to ask the question. It worked! It kept Alec doing his monolog in French, and in return, I shouted, Yes! Very good! *Oui! Très bien!* But after ten minutes, I could not keep up the *charade,* and Alec switched back to English.

With no help from his parents, Alec also learned French by going to an organized French play group Saturday mornings for three hours. To help the minority language, an activity or sport in that language is a bonus. If your community does not offer these type of activities/ language classes, start your own group/meet-up and surround yourself by like-minded people.

Another learning language tip: watching videos/cartoons. Alec is allowed to have "screen time" in the mornings (Monday to Friday) but only in French. I let him watch about twenty minutes while I get ready. In the afternoons, it's his choice - any language he wishes. It's a great tool but nothing can replace a two-way conversation with a real person. By the way, Alec didn't watch any screens until he was almost two years old.

After watching a few German episodes of *Robbi, Tobbi und das Fliewatüüt*, Alec was infatuated for robots. The show is more than a bit outdated (and weird). It's from the 1970's about a little boy and his robot. My husband used to watch it, and he bought the video without my approval. Whatever.

But it led to an interesting way for Alec to grasp the concept of languages and accents. Alec and I would talk like robots (in English), and I read books sometimes in a robot *accent.* Then it gave me the idea to speak Monster language and Alien language with him. Such good learning fun! And he rattles back with the silliest noises.

Oh, if your child is learning French, google *Maurice Chevalier*. I chase Alec around the house with this French accent. It's such a raw, boisterous, hilarious accent.

Trying to make myself feel less guilty, I try to see the benefits of

Alec learning French without mama or papa's help. Maybe he has been so accepting of French because it's his own special language that we do not speak. His little secret; a unique identity and independence from us. Or maybe learning French is an absolute necessity for him; a survival skill. In order to communicate at school, he has no choice but to learn the language.

FULL SPEED AHEAD

Since Alec was two and eight months, I have made him sit at his desk and do age-appropriate activity books with me; teaching him to sit still and concentrate on a task. Also, it allows fifteen to twenty minutes of meaningful, undistracted, one-on-one time together. At three years old, he holds my hand and leads me to his room and asks to do his activity books. It's not like I'm pushing piano lessons like Amy Chua (*the* Tiger Mother) did with her three year old [2] - but secretly I thought long and hard about whether Alec should do the same. Amy Chua used the Suzuki piano books/method for her daughters. [3] I'm thinking of starting Alec with the guitar around the age of five.

I feel we are giving our child ample opportunities. Yes, at two and eight months old we might be expecting more than the average, but we simply want Alec to have more options. I make strides every day that our son will have as many choices as possible. Education prepares us for the unknown and to find our passion in work and life.

I did not become a doctor or a university professor. I don't know if I would have desired to be a lawyer or chemist. I did not attend an Ivy league or any major college. What frustrates me is that I never had the choice. My parents were only able to provide me the educational opportunities that were within their reach.

It was their values and financial capabilities that determined my career path and laid the foundation. I wasn't programed to be *anything you want to be*. There was no room for dreamers or risk takers. They encouraged their children in the areas in which they deemed worthy and where we could secure a comfortable lifestyle. I eventually became a by-product of middle-class-America.

I immensely enjoyed reading Katherine Ellison's book *The Mommy Brain*. Here's a laugh out loud passage about how she prepares her children for the global market. "My mother used to tell us to eat all our vegetables because starving children in China and India didn't have that luxury. I tell my children to study harder, because otherwise children in China and India may grow up to buy and sell them." [4]

PULLING THE EMERGENCY BRAKE

Update: Alec is a little over three years, and I am backpedaling with Alec's activities. I slowed way down on his ability to read, write, simple math, and no more activity books. Well, I still do the activity books but different kinds; only coloring books or cutting out images. Also, no musical instruments until he is in school. I would like for him to test out different instruments, and he can decide which one he wants to play.

What changed? I was thinking more and more about how I lashed out towards Alec because of my personal experiences. Yes, we will still continue to nurture and provide him with the best opportunities; however, I realized I was pushing too much.

Rather than deleting/editing the above part in this chapter, I wanted to show you (the readers) my thought process. Everything is not so simple, and I make mistakes. I have made a lot of mistakes, but I learn, correct and move forward.

Making Alec sit down with me at his little table while I persuaded him to trace letters, be incredibly persistent on following the instructions, or giving him check marks and X's was way too early. I began to see how disappointed he would get if I gave him an X for getting a task wrong. I stopped this immediately. And I saw how unnatural it is for such a young child to sit at a desk. Now I let him color standing up, laying down or on his head. His teachers can tell him to stay in the lines. That doesn't have to be my job.

I have drastically cut back on teaching Alec how to read and write. I think he can handle it but concentrating on his fluency of German and French is more time critical before the age of six years old. [5] I am not too concerned with Alec's fluency of English. I am a talker, and I talk a lot with Alec. Alec seldom asks the question "Why?" because I explain everything. We have an ample amount of time together so naturally his English is fine.

I still practice letter sounds with Alec. For example, I continue to use the blending method, but again, I slowed way down on this, too. I decided that this should occur in the classroom. Also, I want him to learn math from his teachers. For Alec's situation, I thought it is best for him to learn in a classroom environment and let the teachers/school system decide the appropriate time to begin. This new way of thinking on my part was mostly due because of Germany's and Finland's philosophy of education - to start formal education at six or seven years. Many other countries are looking to start later and add more playtime.

What also changed was that Jens and I both realized what a perfectionist Alec was becoming. Alec is a typical normal kid for his age, but it's something that caught our attention. I just kind of readjusted how I react to Alec when he doesn't do something correctly.

I communicate with him a lot more on how things don't turn how we expected or that we mess up sometimes. We are human. We make mistakes. It's more important how we react and adjust to those mistakes. Will we learn and grow from them? Or will we sulk and be frustrated?

Before you (the readers) begin to think I am some terribly overbearing mother, I would like to share a story that hopefully illustrates what kind of parent I am. I am not a parent that teaches out of fire and brimstone but out of love.

Recently, Alec was at a physical therapy appointment - nothing major. After a few appointments, the physical therapist (German mom of four) commented on how positive and encouraging I am with Alec. She went off on a tangent, and I thought for a moment that she was criticizing me.

"What do you mean?" I said.

"I notice you are always encouraging him. You have such positive things to say," said the physical therapist.

"So you are saying it is a good thing, right?" I said.

Now she is laughing.

"Oh, yes! I think it's wonderful. I have been doing this (physical therapy for children) for thirty years, and I think it is so important for children to hear. It's not so common here in Germany," therapist.

"Positive words of encouragement are not so common?" me.

"Yes, but not like how you do it. I believe children need to hear these supportive words from their parents, but I think Germans don't say it as much as they should," therapist.

I pause. I am a little shocked. I am a little sad. I don't know how to respond. She grasps this and continues to praise me about how I give Alec so much positive reinforcement. At that moment, I picked up

Alec and gave him a big hug. Even though he was getting really heavy, I felt the weight of the world lifted off me.

FRENCH COMPETENCE

"He speaks in complete sentences, and he understands everything I say," remarked Alec's French play tutor (Nathalie L. Brochard). She said this after his first private lesson when he was three years and seven months old. I had no idea his French was so good! From this point, I began telling everyone Alec is trilingual.

In the past year since Alec started at Lycée, Jens and I didn't know his French language capabilities. Alec did receive approval for Alec to advance from *petit section* to *moyenne section*. And we received a comprehensive evaluation report with grades. These do not count until he starts proper school (compulsory). It showed below average marks in French. I was gutted until I turned a few pages to his German grades. They were not pretty either. The next day I asked the parents in his class about their children's grades. Many of them had the same as Alec! And their kid(s) are native French speakers! Well, at least one of their parents speaks French.

A few parents explained to me that the French grading system is harsh. But the parent's soothing, relaxed demeanor did not quite ease my conscience. May is their end of year and instead of doing the sensible thing like asking for a meeting with Alec's head caregiver, I panicked and hired Nathalie as a 'tutor'. I didn't want a meeting with Alec's teacher because she only speaks French. And with her limited German - mostly mine - it's always painful to communicate with her.

Jens and I had scheduled a meeting with her mid-way through the school year, but when we showed up, she didn't. She was out sick. Jens was annoyed he had missed a morning of work, and we never rescheduled. Also, none of Alec's caregivers never mentioned he was struggling with French or recommend that we get extra help. Plus, Alec had been going to a Saturday morning French play group since he turned three years old. It's basically a big playdate without the parents. There's one caregiver to ten children, and they simply encourage the kids to play in French. This fun little group follows the natural way young children should learn, "through play, social interaction and participation." [6] The NAEYC (National Association for the Education of Young Children) encourages this play-based style of learning, too. [7] I apply this logic while hunting for native speaking babysitters.

We want Alec to learn French by playing; not with flashcards. Here's my ad that I posted in a French speaking Facebook group in Hamburg. I posted it in English and French using Google translator. I ran the same ad again when Alec began Spanish. Obviously, parents should tailor it to their requirements, for example, maybe you need someone three times a week.

Hello! We are looking for a French speaking babysitter. Someone to spend 2 hours per week with our three-year-old son. Just playing and reading some books (I have French books). The MOST important thing is that the person speaks a lot with him. For your information, he is trilingual in German, English and French. This job is open to adults and students.
Location is in (insert city or area) and near (insert public transportation stop).
Monday or Tuesday or Friday afternoons from 14:00 - 16:00 or 15:00 - 17:00
This job is available for once or twice a week for 2 hours each time.
Thank you! I will check my "other" Facebook message box.

After I received a message from a potential babysitter, I followed it up with this message individually in English and the target language.

Hello! Thanks for responding.
I am using Google translator. I hope the translation is ok.
As I said…I am looking for someone to play, read and talk (in French only) with our son. No formal teaching experience is necessary and no lesson plans.
What schedule works best for you?
And what would you charge per hour?
Thank you,
Marlane

Here's a tip, when it comes to searching for a babysitter to learn or nurture a language, post an ad on the internet. Don't waste your time like I did with putting up flyers. Even with flyers at Lycée, it didn't land me a babysitter! I asked several teachers directly if they wanted the job, too. Finally, one suggested I post in the French speaking Hamburg Facebook group. In a matter of 24 hours, I received several replies versus spending a month of frustration and stress with those stupid flyers.

I was incredibly happy with the responses, and the prices per hour were reasonable. However, the best part was that one of Alec's caregivers at Le Petit Monde replied to my Facebook post. I had known her for six months but never asked her. I initially wrote her off thinking she would charge too much but no!

Jens and I are thankful for Nathalie. And it worked out for Alec since he already knew her. But even not knowing Alec's Spanish babysitter before, he took to her very quickly. At the end of the first babysitting session, Alec gave her a big hug and walked her out.

When Nathalie explained to me that Alec is fluent in French, we agreed she should continue with Alec so he can have two way conversations. He certainly does not receive one-on-one attention at Lycée and needs more opportunities to speak and improve/expand his vocabulary. And Jens and I cannot provide this to him either so, a native speaking tutor/babysitter it shall be! Additionally, she reads a lot of books to him.

I never imagined my child speaking three languages; excuse me, four - more on that later. Of course marrying a German I knew he would be bilingual. There were two main things that happened which convinced us that Alec should learn a third language.

First, how early Alec became bilingual. He was not a gifted baby or toddler. He didn't show remarkable capabilities. As a baby and toddler, he was average/normal. However, Jens and I were in shock of Alec's speech and understanding of German and English at such an early age. All the books, blogs, articles and studies say that before the age of three this is completely normal. But it's difficult not to be amazed by your toddler speaking two languages. Until you experience it first hand, it's hard to grasp.

When Alec easily became bilingual, we thought, *He knows two languages at such an early age...why not add a third?*

The second reason why we wanted Alec to learn a third language is Jens' limitations at work. Airbus is a global company, and English is the business language at multi-international companies. Jens' English is excellent; beyond excellent as a non-native speaker. But within the higher-ranking management community at Airbus, it's imperative to speak French. Of course it's not a requirement just an unspoken truth.

Ok, Alec does not have to work at Airbus. He can choose whatever career path he so desires. Like I stated in the last chapter, we want to provide him with the most choices in order to give him more opportunities. And languages are extremely powerful and important tools. Some reasons to learn French:

- One of the six official languages at United Nations (applications for work are available in English and French)
- Helpful in the European Parliament/Council
- Working at Airbus or any other global company
- Economic opportunities in west Africa if it continues to become more politically stable
- The France Diplomatie also has a great list: http://www.diplomatie.gouv.fr/en/french-foreign-policy/

francophony/promoting-french-around-the-world-7721/article/10-good-reasons-for-learning

STARTING BEFORE THREE YEARS OLD

Before I even read the book *Trilingual by Six* by Lennis Dipper MD, Alec was already attending the French daycare at Lycée. He was well on his way to learning his third language, and we had a set plan of action. But reading the book confirmed and explained all the reasons for immersing children in different languages. I stumbled upon this treasure by researching related topics. I highly recommend it on raising a bilingual, trilingual or multilingual child.

One of the stronger points that Dr. Dippel makes is to introduce non-native languages by the age of three if not before. The linguist guru Noam Chomsky discovered that children have a "language acquisition device" until the age of about three years old to learn language(s), and then it starts to fade. [8] Chomsky theorized that babies/toddlers learn languages because it is a type of survival skill. This language acquisition device in infants and young children's brains is "designed not for speech itself but for the *acquisition* of speech and learning to understand the spoken word." [9] This is why it's so much easier for children to learn languages than as adults.

Dr. Dippel also uses different studies to support why languages should be started before the age of three. He lists twelve in one chapter. In my opinion, the most hard data is the study by Kovelman, Baker and Petitto in 2008 using functional neuroimaging. "In the relatively new field of functional neuroimaging, where the brain's electrical activity can be viewed with special scanners from moment to moment, scientists have found that when a child learns a second language before the age of 3, the brain processes it in the say way as the first language. If a child acquires a second language after the age of 3, however, the pattern of brain activity is more chaotic and decentralized." [10]

It was pure luck that Alec started at his French daycare before the age of three. Jens and I had know idea of all the benefits and studies proving that it's best to start before the age of three. The only reason we started Alec so early is because his birthday is in December. We actually wanted him to start a year later; however, the Lycée administration would not budge. He had to start the year he turned three. He was the youngest one in his class and many of the children were almost a full year older (and a head taller) than him given that his birthday is so late in the year.

ALEC'S FRENCH PROGRESS

3 years and 9 months:

When Alec plays by himself, it is mostly in French. Of course when I play with him, he switches to English and German with his papa. But when it is his own independent play time, he is talking/ narrating in French.

3 years and 10 months:

Alec's head caregiver/teacher at Lycée casually mentioned to me that Alec's French is very good. I froze. I somehow managed to let out a soft *merci*. Then Alec pulled my arm for us to catch up with his friends. I stumbled over my Hamburg rain boots and regained my composure. The same week another teacher came up to me and reiterated, "I heard Alec speaking French the other day, and it was very good."

3 years and 11 months:

Around this time on a Monday, Alec insisted…I mean *insisted* that his friend from his daycare/class come over. The girl's mother said that she needed to run some errands and couldn't do today. Alec and his girlfriend pleaded (and screamed) that she should come over. I nervously suggested to the mom, "Is it ok if she comes home with us? I can bring her home in a couple of hours." It would be the first time we had one of his friends stay without the mom. She agreed and off the children went running with smiles the size of the Grand Canyon.

The following day when I picked up Alec from Lycée the same thing happened. But I explained to Alec that she could not come over everyday to our place. He cried the entire way home. I felt so awful that the next day we invited her over again, and she happily came without her mom. What a great little couple these two make! They play so nicely, and it's intriguing to listen to them play together. Sometimes they speak in French and sometimes in German - the girl does not know any English. They will talk in French for maybe fifteen minutes and then switch to German for five minutes and then back to French but not mixing the languages. I notice they don't frequently switch French and German. Also, another great opportunity for Alec to practice French.

I have always worried if Alec would mix languages when he got a bit older. For example, in one sentence if he would use both German and English or if he would throw in a French word while he speaks in English. Nope. Never. I think it came from using OPOL (one parent one language). Also having a clear, set boundary while learning French at Lycée.

4 years:

Dr. Dippel wrote the book *Trilingual by Six*. Alec was trilingual by four. Jens and I are overwhelmingly proud of our son. But I am also proud of us as parents. I thought giving him two passports were the greatest gifts we could give him. No, giving him the opportunity to learn multiple languages is by far the greatest gifts.

A third native speaking French teacher came up to me at Lycée and complimented Alec's French. It was just before we went on Christmas vacation. Bashfully, I thanked her. Receiving that compliment was my favorite Christmas gift.

ON BECOMING MULTILINGUAL

How we came to the conclusion on a fourth language was mostly due to reading the book *Trilingual by Six*. After I read the could-not-put-it-down book in three days, I gave it to Jens to read. He didn't even put up a fight. As soon as I mentioned that Noam Chomsky is referenced in the book, it was downloaded in seconds. I couldn't believe how easy it was to convince Jens that our son could and should learn a fourth language. So, when Alec was three years and nine months old, we hired a Spanish babysitter.

How I found Alec's native Spanish speaking tutor/babysitter was the exact same way I found his French one. I posted in a Spanish Facebook group in Hamburg and received an overwhelmingly huge response within 24 hours. After Alec's first two-hour play lesson, I asked Alejandra how it went. She said even though Alec is a beginner, he understood a lot. Of course French and Spanish have many similar words. Also, she pointed out that he is very good about rolling the Spanish letter "R". Eureka! That's right! Because Alec has a native French accent, he mastered the Spanish "R" instantly. Fascinating.

For the past few months, Alejandra has only come over once a week for two hours each time. Since I have been hearing so much praise of Alec's French progress, I feel comfortable to add more Spanish hours; whether it be from a babysitter, scheduled playdates or a private play/activity class held in Spanish. At this time, Alec barely knows any Spanish. But when Alejandra asks him a simple question in Spanish, Alec responds with the correct answer in English or French. This was only meant to introduce the language and for him to be aware of another language.

Although Alec is not fluent in Spanish - yet, when someone asks him what languages he speaks, he responds, "Engl-*ish*, German, French and a little Span-*ish*."

LANGUAGE QUOTES & A PLEA

To all the parents, teachers, caregivers, principals, school board members, state superintendents and policymakers in the world: language is value. And I hope you implement languages into our children's education.

Here are my favorite language quotes:

Language is a city to the building of which every human being brought a stone.
Ralph Waldo Emerson

To have another language is to possess a second soul.
Charlemagne

The individual's whole experience is built upon the plan of his language.
Henri Delacroix

If we spoke a different language, we would perceive a somewhat different world.
Ludwig Wittgenstein

Those who know nothing of foreign languages know nothing of their own.
Johann Wolfgang von Goethe

If you talk to a man in a language he understands, that goes to his head. If you talk to him in his own language, that goes to his heart.
Nelson Mandela

A BIG MULTICULTURAL GROUP HUG

Natural resources are "the natural wealth of a country, consisting of land, forests, mineral deposits, water, ect." [11]

My natural resources are the diverse set of parents that makeup the *village* that help us raise Alec and all the children in our community. We all share an obligation that is of the most importance. Yes, I would have survived the early years without them, but in sharing tears of laughter and pain, I have found more happiness.

This section documents parenting tips that my international crowd have so graciously supplied. *Thank you for your generosity and friendship* ~

But first, an interesting by-product resulted from asking my friends to share their best parenting tip. I also asked them a follow-up question of where the tip originated from. For example, maybe their mother, a book/blog or perhaps it's a tradition in their country - word on the street. Then the question would expand to *where are you from?*

However when I asked the question *where are you from?,* I always felt a sense of uncomfortableness asking this question. *Is it politically incorrect to ask?* I couldn't put my finger on it. I realized that the question was ok to ask - sort of - but something was missing.

How does one fully answer this question? How can one answer with simply saying, for example in my case, *American*? I am American, but my experiences and even the certain time periods I lived in those places is where I am truly from. For example, *my* New York City is of the nitty-gritty Hells Kitchen era. The time before Disney swept in and bought all of Times Square. When Manhattan was a melting pot and I rented a room for 600 dollars on the Upper West Side. My five years in Manhattan were about misfit nights and seeing unforeseen fortunes like the poetry slams at the Nuyorican in Alphabet City. A time when it was "do or die Bed-Stuy" not hipsters sporting man-beards gentrifying every crevice of the BK. Now it's conversations about hedge funds and the 1%.

My other five years I spent in Astoria, Queens. This is where the Greeks, Albanians, Bosnians, Croatians and Serbians all lived peacefully together while back in their homelands, they fought each other. But in Astoria, we shared the love of borek, hummus, baklava, mom & pop coffee shops and a beer at the Czech/Slovak Bohemian Beer Garden.

I grew up in a small Texas *town* when the population was 12,000 people. Now there is more than 60,000 people, and the *city* will be 100% powered by renewable energy by 2017. *What? Wow!* I was raised two miles outside town. Now the NAFTA (North American Free Trade Agreement) Superhighway runs through where my back-corner bedroom use to be. There were a few peach trees and a garden that got cursed under my mother's breathe. Well, she used the word *dern* while pulling weeds and shooing away critters and bugs. The government bulldozed the house and took the land by eminent domain for a toll road.

What is your ethnicity/background? How should I answer that question? I am a 12th American-generation Wingo, and from my mother's side, I am eighth generation. America opened her arms to all immigrants and was a melting pot from the very beginning. Am I Dutch, English, Italian and Irish? I'm not sure if I am Native American/First Nation. Could there be some Scottish? How much? Maybe I have a bit of French maybe not. Who knows? Who cares? We do care because we ask the question. We constantly ask the question when meeting someone new. It's a way to start a conversation. It's a way to get to know someone. But you don't get to know someone with this closed-ended question.

I was raised in Texas. I lived in NYC, southern California and Hamburg. But these places don't include all the diverse people that I have shared experiences, and their cultural traits I picked up from them. It doesn't come close. So what does that make me? Where am I from?

There can be dangerous consequences in saying where one is from.

It leads to stereotypes, judgement or a power struggle between people. [12] When someone asks me, *Where are you from?*, I say *Austin, Texas,* but quickly follow it up with *but I lived in New York for ten years* - hoping the person won't put me in a box as a gun swinging, Bush lovin', radical right-wing Texan. My go to answer use to be New York City, but then Austin got discovered as the southern San Francisco. So, I feel comfortable with declaring Austin, Texas, but emphasizing the word Austin.

After watching Taiye Selasi's TED talk, *Don't ask where I'm from, ask where I'm a local*, I decided I needed a game changer response. Taiye stresses the importance of knowing that we are all multi-layered, multi-ethnic and our human experiences define us; not the myth of national identity. I love her response to the misguided, misinterpreted, and in some cases, politically incorrect question. In her talk, she expresses that by answering *I'm a multi-local* has more truth than stating a country because countries are invented and constantly changing.

I am answering, "A little bit of everywhere," and leaving it as an open-ended answer. I figure if someone wants to know more I'll tell them my story. I don't enjoy being compartmentalized.

As for asking the proper question to find out where one is from, maybe it's best not to ask in the beginning. In my opinion, rather to respect the person's privacy at a safe distance until you get the feeling they are ok with you asking, and they can share their story.

FIELD RESEARCH

Tips from my friends around the globe by topic are listed below. I simply asked these two questions:

#1 What parenting tip would you like to share?
#2 Where or how did you get this tip?

It was completely up to them how they wished to respond. For example, some gave a specific tip or tool. Others shared an emotional/psychological tip. Most tips I received are pretty universal and knowing the story behind *where are you from* for each parent could get pretty lengthy. But in some cases, I thought it was funny or interesting to add it.

Routines

Anything you want to change in your kid's routine. For example, feeding, bed time, sleeping habits, try it for a week maximum and if your kid resists the change, go back to the way it was before and try again a couple of weeks later.

~ Advice from a German midwife

Bedtime Routine

"But I don't want to get ready for bed!" What parent hasn't heard this exclamation a million times? Explain to your child that you will read them three books before going to bed. But every time they act up, while doing their bedtime routine, one less book will be read.

Dressing for Cold Weather

If your little darling protests not to wear a jacket on a cold day, then let them experience the cold bite on their own. As soon as they step outside, they will beg for their jacket.

~ Canadian parent Whitney

Eating

To avoid picky eating later, use baby led weaning. This concept is from Gill Rapley, author of *Baby-led Weaning*. She explains that babies don't have to be spoon-fed and self-feeding is the best way for your child to become a healthy eater.

(*If I had the opportunity to do it over again, I would definitely read this book.*)

Sleeping

When a baby is sleeping, don't be too quiet. That way they learn to sleep with some noise, and it allows for better sleep. We did this with our daughter, and she's a champion sleeper. She was rough at first like most kiddos, but we were consistent with her routines, and we didn't do anything overly complicated to get her to sleep.

I don't know about the rest of the world, but in Germany, the book *The Rabbit Who Wants To Fall Asleep* by Swedish author Carl-Johan Forssén Ehrlin is very popular. I thought it was a gimmick, but a friend really kept recommending it. I tried it on my four year old, and in a few minutes, she fell asleep in her father's arms.

Parenting Ideologies

Do what works. Sometimes following an ideology like attachment parenting makes us too inflexible and everyone suffers. If crying it out works for your family, do that. If co-sleeping works, do that.

Enjoy this time because they grow up so fast! Also, people said to me, "Don't carry your baby too much because he/she will get spoiled and want to be held all the time." It's a lie! Also, I took lots of naps with my baby in my bed. Since he was six months old, he has slept in his bed and bedroom without any problems. There is no rule! You need to feel what you love is best for your baby.

The utmost importance is to keep alive the emotional connection with your child.

Kids learn almost purely by example. If you want to teach them something, you have to lead by example. Otherwise, they will just copy what you really do.

Realize from day one that your child is their own person. Always try to be respectful of them and their wishes. Work together with them rather than trying to impose how you want them to act or what you want them to do.

If you plan to do something, never expect it to go as you thought. Don't always hold on to the original plan when you notice your child wants to try something else. It's better to let them go for it once in a while. It will be much more relaxing than forcing them to go to some course/class they don't want to participate in. Sometimes the child needs to feel you take their ideas seriously.

Be patient.

Toilet Training

A mom from Burkina Faso (country in West Africa) told me that toilet training *where she comes from* starts much earlier. She compares it to her experiences with the German daycares and parents in

Hamburg. She started putting her daughter and son on a small toilet when they were one year old.

Spontaneity or Make Plans?

I used to be spontaneous. I didn't have all these set plans. But after living in Germany for some time, and especially after having children, I realized that it's good to make plans. Of course, with children, it doesn't always happen. Don't get upset or disappointed when events/plans don't work out.

Problems = Solutions

Sometimes the most helpful thing you can give your child is simply to get down on the floor and play with your baby/toddler. They are begging for your attention and want nothing more than to please you.

(I have found this to be so true! Sometimes I am not actively playing with Alec, but I am present; intermittently laying lifelessly on Alec's stuffed animal named Mr. Moo Moo or using his books as a makeshift pillow.)

Always share with other parents who have similar aged children when experiencing a problem or some new issue. Can also find help in Facebook groups or educators from daycare.

I would like to add my favorite parenting tip here. When you have found a solution/great parenting advice; share it within your village. Also, share it with the world via social media or whatever outlet you desire! Sharing is caring!

~ Marlane

Discipline

For those rough times, pick your battles. As in, you'll go nuts if you try to do everything. Pick the most important things you want to work on with your child and start with those.

"Three strikes and you are out." Meaning, give three warnings with explaining the consequence(s) and then follow through. Basically, being consistent with what you say has helped us loads.

Kids don't do anything to annoy you. They do things for childish reasons. They mean no harm. Treat them with respect and most of all LOVE! No matter what they have done.

If you want your children to do something and they refuse…if you have time, let them do it a little later without nagging them. Then ask them kindly to do what you want. And continuously repeat it every time more firm and serious. Don't snap at them instantly, they will not understand.

TIPS FROM PARENTS WITH THREE CHILDREN

Stick to your "No" or say it's an exception.

When children quarrel, don't take sides or else it is a never ending story. Scold both children, one for starting it and the other for responding to the fight. And then separate the two kids.

Always teach children to be polite; someday it will be natural to say please and thank you.

Don't argue or try to reason with children who are tired. Just ignore them and drive/get home. They will whine and cry at everything anyway.

I am not a friend. I am the mum. I am the Boss. At least that's what I always tell them while they do whatever they want.

Depending on their age, don't ask too much of them. Bombarding children with several options is what German parents do.

Sing with and for them. The same goes for reading.

Depending on the child's character, try not to rant and shout (though that's what you really want to do). Sooth your voice, embrace them and say, "I'm listening now. Tell me why did you react that way?"

Always make them responsible for their actions. If they messed up; face the consequences. I will scold like hell, but love you know matter what and stand by you.

Finally, remember you love those little buggers.

�֍⸙֍⸙֍⸙֍⸙֍

My parenting tip is go with your motherly instincts. God gave them to you for a reason. It's good to get advice and opinions of everyone around (because they will always give it to you), but then go with what you feel is best for you and your child. You are the child's mom, and you are the one that knows best. It may not be the norm or what everyone has told you, but it will be right because you are doing what is best for you and your child. I formed this tip on my own. When I had my first child, I got so much advice from friends, family, nurses, books, etc, which I loved but, at times, I had to go against everything everyone had said because of what I felt was right for my own child.

From day one, slow down the care giving moments to make them a time of connection. Slow down the rhythm when you change a diaper, slow down the bath time, feeding time, brushing teeth. All these care giving moments that seem sometimes transitional before moving to the next step or before doing something meaningful together with your child, for example, playing together or drawing. Instead of perceiving the diaper change as a "must do" moment before doing something more important, I would say that this is the important moment. This should be the moment of connection, and then off your child goes to play.

Play is a child's job. It's his field which you can join when you choose. But the love, affection and connection should happen in the care giving moments where we should stay focused and slow it down; make it a big important moment of showing our love. And when the child has taken his does of love, and he can go back to what he was doing happily before. Now you can go back to work, cooking or dealing with the next child. If the child resists or is having a melt down, then slow it down even more. I got this tip from the child expert Magda Gerber, her book, *Dear Parent: Caring for Infants With*

Respect. She is known for R.I.E. (Resources for Infant Educarers) - it's about treating babies with respect and trust.

When we travel long distances with the kids, the Trip Wizard (parent) will leave random inexpensive gifts in the child's carry on or car seat. It's usually something like a sticker book or Play Doh. It has worked well for us keeping the kids occupied, and they love the anticipation of when a gift will show up. I met a flight attendant at one of my husband's work functions who recommended we try this for a our first overseas flight. It was a big hit, and it stuck. Now the kids look forward to traveling.

My number one tip is to be consistent and to follow-through on your words. Consistency helps kids understand what is happening next and gives a measure of security. Follow-through is equally important. If you tell your child that if he hits his sister, he can not watch television. Then follow-through on the punishment. Likewise, if you promised a treat or chocolate, make sure you do that as well.

When you make a mistakes along the way, don't be afraid to tell your child, "Hey, I made a mistake, and I'm really sorry."

The last thing is to be present. It is fine to have time when you are checking messages and connecting with others, but have times during the day like meals, reading books or other times when you set rules that everyone is electronic free and be present as a family. If you start that when they are young, hopefully you can follow-through with it as they get older.

THIRTY MINUTES OF PURE BLISS

Another thing that saves parents are playpens. Parents, if you wish to take a shower on a daily basis, buy a playpen. There will be tears in the beginning, but it's ok. Everything will be ok. Ok? Ok.

One has to gradually increase the minutes day by day to reach the desired amount of time. For example, when babies learn how to do their tummy time. They slowly gain their strength and confidence little by little.

Place your darling in the playpen for a few minutes at a time and progressively build up to thirty minutes. Yes! Thirty minutes! Since Alec started *kita* (at one year), I put Alec in his playpen from 8:00 to 8:30am. Or parents can start as early as six months or seven months. [13] Just be sure to place them in when they are fresh and alert so, they don't fall asleep. The toys/objects could be sleeping hazards. [14]

I was able to take a shower, dress and even had time for makeup. Parents can get a lot done in thirty minutes if you are not preoccupied with a little one. This time was my serenity. I miss that playpen.

Alec always gave a whiney whimper about going into his playpen. But I wouldn't stress out because I knew he would quickly settle down and play with his favorite toys that were strategically placed inside. And it's a safe place for independent play. [15] Of course I would check in on him a few times but never letting him see me.

When Alec was around twenty months old, I stopped putting him in the playpen during my morning routine. It got to the point where he could climb out. But use it as long as your darling will stay put in it! [16] He was (and still is) happy to play with a toy or read a book on the bathroom rug while I shower and get ready so, I can still keep an eye on him. But there are unwanted objects that get dropped in the shower. He loves to hand me things like my towel and Q-tips.

Even Jo Frost of *Supernanny* recommends playpens! Great for play but overuse does mean neglect. [17]

What to do without a playpen? Instead of a blissful shower, there is an alternative: dry shampoo and baby wipes. Not as nice as a deep soak in a tub while listening to Sarah McLachlan.

We also have another confined area for Alec; a crib in the kitchen. We lowered the mattress to the bottom position. Our friends have twins, and they gave them to us when they outgrew their cribs. I didn't want to take both of them, but she insisted that we would use them. "Have one in his bedroom and put the other somewhere in the house. You'll be able to get some work done." Boy, oh boy, was she right.

As soon as Alec started crawling, I asked Jens to put the extra crib in the kitchen since we already had the playpen in the living room.

"In the kitchen? Are you sure?" Jens.

"Yes, we're in there a lot," me.

"When are we in the kitchen? I don't think very often," Jens.

"What?! Really?! You don't think we are in the kitchen very often?" me.

"Well, I don't think a crib is meant to be in the kitchen," Jens.

"Why not?" me.

"Because it doesn't go in a kitchen. You cook and eat in there," Jens. The typical German response of there always being a time and a place for everything.

"But that's why I want it in the kitchen. I can't look after Alec when I need to pay attention to boiling water and sharp knives laying on the counter. I don't want him crawling around on the floor. I could trip over him," me.

This went on for another good ten minutes. One would think we were debating the next presidential election. It finally ended with me saying, "Please, Jens, let's leave it in here for a couple of days. If you don't think it is useful in here, we can take it out." It stayed for over a year in the kitchen.

When Alec began to walk, we replaced the crib with a plastic child table and chair. I prefer wood furniture but not in this case. I scrub down the table and chair in the bathtub. Easy peasy. Not only did Alec like to eat his meals there, he loved to push the plastic chair all through the house. Only fell over it twice. Ouchie!

Just when we thought we were done with the second crib, I had yet another brilliant idea. Alec was outgrowing his sleeping crib so, I thought we could combine the two since they are exactly the same. It worked! Jens simply removed one side of the cribs, and we used plastic ties - cable/zip ties to hold them together. When Alec turned two, Jens sawed off five of the end bars so, Alec could crawl in and out of his bed without rolling out during the night.

Whenever Alec is roaming around the house, unsupervised, I occasionally call out, "Alec, are you ok!?" It's a good way to reassure both of us. Around three years old, I learned of a similar follow-up tip. When your child doesn't answer the first time, the parent calls out something like "Alec, check." [18] Then he answers back "Mama, check." If no answer, then it's time to make a mad dash around the house.

At almost four years, Alec stopped replying all together. I had to re-strategize. At the time, he was obsessed with a cartoon called Fireman Sam. While in the shower - where many of my brilliant ideas are formed, I conceived another way to get a response.

I came out of the shower and yelled, "Firefighter Alec, check!"

~ long pause ~

"Firefighter Mama, check!" Alec.

THE TERRIBLE THREES

Brace yourself, we have arrived at the Terrible Threes. Welcome to H - E - double L.

Although I believe strongly in a designated bad-behavior corner or stair-step, it's going to take more to discipline this strong-willed, emotional roller coaster three year old. I don't care what all the snuggly, warm toddler experts say.

First, I always try the corner. It that doesn't work then I send him to his bedroom to calm down. Last resort: I call papa at work.

When I tell Alec *I'm calling papa*, this sets off fire sirens. Alec knows that I have reached my breaking point and summoned the big artillery. I rarely call Jens at work. It can wait until he gets home. However, it is completely unacceptable for any child to hit or push mama with great force. FULL STOP. And with a few phone calls over a month's time. It was out of Alec's system. Now for the next round: lying.

Thank goodness this phase didn't last long because we nipped it in the bud right from the beginning. Our precious little angel started the game of *mama said...papa said...*, "Papa said I could have a cookie or mama said I don't have to brush my teeth." Outright lies. But I always give Alec the option to tell the truth; a last attempt to come clean. If not, then drastic measures are taken, and I say to him, *I'm calling papa.*

I feel hitting and lying are the two single worst acts of behavior. Whatever you find the most appalling should be dealt with immediately and with significant punishment. For Alec, this is having papa's disapproval.

Alec gets panic-stricken when he knows papa is upset with him. Alec isn't scared rather it creates kind of a distraught sadness in him. Alec sees his father - like most fathers - as a hero who can do no wrong. When I have to call Jens at work, Alec knows as soon as papa walks through that door, papa is going to have a firm, heart to heart discussion about his misbehavior (absolutely no physical punishment). After a couple of weeks of not telling the truth, it slowed way down, and Alec grasped the severity of lying.

My other go-to tool resulting from bad behavior, but not as severe as lying and hitting, is no videos/screen time. But I don't just tell Alec. I write in on a post-it note and stick it to his door. This physical act of writing it down makes it more believable to him. Also, when he asks to watch more videos - and he is not allowed to - I take his hand and march him to his door. I read the post-it note to remind him of his bad behavior.

For less harsh behavior, I resort to a few Jedi mind tricks; one of them being distractions. For example, when it's time to turn off *the screen*. I know this is a tantrum in the making. One time I said to Alec, "I heard robots in the bathroom. We better turn off the video and go look for them!" But try to do this before a tantrum flairs up. [19] Once that bull gets going, it will break all the china in the shop.

And then there's choices. Let them feel like they are part of the decision making process. [20] When Alec requests something ridiculous as a snack like ice-cream, I hammer back, "You may have a yogurt or a banana." This does not work 99.9% of the time. So then I follow it up with, "You have three choices. A yogurt, a banana or nothing." Repeat two more times.

I have also found that bending down and talking to Alec at eye-level helps. Clear communication in tantrum situations is imperative. [21] I need to understand him, and he needs to understand me. No matter how out of control the little beast erupts, try to stay calm but firm.

I know some parents resort to pacifiers to help subdue a tantrum. But, please, for the love of your child, get rid of the thing before their adult teeth come in around the age of five. [22] More appropriately, no pacifier beyond the age of two - at the very latest. [23]

Alec never had a problem of his nightly routine of brushing his teeth. Also, washing his hair was not a big deal until the glorious age of three. For months, we battled and negotiated with him. But I did find an instant solution to one of the problems after complaining to a German mother about him refusing to brush his teeth. She suggested I tell Alec that there are trolls living in his mouth that hammer away on his teeth with a pick ax. The trolls also build houses in between the teeth when one doesn't brush. It's the story of Karius and Baktus by the Norwegian author Thorbjørn Egner. Even my husband remembers this story when he was young.

That evening Alec resisted again. The little trolls popped in my head, but I hadn't read the story yet. I quickly made up my own version.

"Alec, we have to brush your teeth because there are monsters in there," I said convincingly.

His ears perked up. I had his attention!

"Come on, let's go brush out those silly monsters playing in your teeth," I said.

I blinked, and he was gone. I found him standing on his bathroom stool with his toothbrush in his hand. This time he was waiting for me.

He brushed his teeth while I narrated, "Get that purple monster in the back! Oh, here's a furry one hiding up top. Silly monster! Ok, let's spit out all those silly monsters in the sink. Rinse real good so, we get them all."

Alas there will be times when nothing seems to work but to adhere to your three year old's demands. Once, and only once because I learned my lesson, I peeled off the lid to Alec's soy yogurt lid. He had a nervous breakdown. I had to scotch tape the stupid lid back on, so he could do it. Oh, and I made the mistake of putting the spoon in the yogurt. I got Alec a clean spoon. Wrong again. Through all his tears, I realized that he wanted the original spoon but cleaned. There was nothing special about the first spoon from the second I offered. It's the same stupid silverware.

HOW TO GET YOUR KID OUT THE DOOR

This problem could be a separate book in itself. I was starting to think of drastic measures like in the German fairy tale book, *Der Struwwelpeter*. The only solution I had for getting Alec out the door in the mornings was by threatening him with no cartoons.

I once again turned to my *village* for help. I posted in the same expat mother Facebook group looking for parents to share their stories and tips. Here's my post, and the following are the comments I received:

"Title of my next book: *HOW TO GET YOUR KID OUT THE DOOR* Now if I only knew how to do it. Starting to think of drastic measures like in the scary German book perhaps a good parenting guide. Suggestions Moms? The only thing that works for us is that I threaten my almost 4 year old with no cartoons for the rest of the day."
~ Marlane Wingo

Facebook Comments:

Hahaha you're so funny Marlane! At home we use the phrase 'In 5 minutes' a lot.. it was actually started by papa and it's been working pretty well for us mostly.. if Eric gets a little warning before it's time to go he knows he gets '5 more minutes' to play or whatever and then it's go time! (Of course not saying everything works perfectly every time but it helps).
* (Marlane Wingo) My response = That's freaking amazing. That has yet to work for us. Hahaha! (Sigh)
* Mom's response = Oh you only have to repeat and repeat and repeat yourself, 100 times, you know, as you do with kids!

I would buy that book! The Christmas advent calendar reward system is helping at the moment, but who knows what we'll do in January.

Ha!! That is too funny. I guess I do the threat thing as well, but I phrase it instead as "let's leave now (or in 5 mins), so there's time for xxx." Works better in the summer when we can get an ice cream on the way back! As with anything with kids though, it doesn't have a 100% success rate alas

At the *kita,* we have a large sand timer which we use so the kids can see the time is passing. At one point we had 3 different timers so the kids could set themselves a target of improvement, e.g from needing 10 min to 5 mins. Haven't personally tried it at home but why not?

Haha! It's what Marcus grew up on (the scary German book) and loves it even today. I've made my kids dress en route...so shove them out the door and make them do everything else as we rush to school

I saw this blog today, perhaps it's the answer? http:// kidsactivitiesblog.com/.../dont-listen-in-the-morning

* (Marlane Wingo) My response = Ok, so the playing for 20 minutes thing is good - getting up earlier.

* (Marlane Wingo) My response to everyone in the thread = Ok. Get this. Today, I had a doctor appointment and they told me not to eat or drink anything. So no coffee this morning for me! BUT...in a weird way....it helped me stay so calm and relaxed! I didn't have a short fuse and fly off the handle in a whim. My son was still being his annoying self when it was time to go to *kita*, but my heart didn't race and I DIDN'T YELL AT HIM ONE TIME! I can't believe. I just ignored him and kind of shuffled him out the door (like on mom suggested in the above Facebook thread). Yeah, so nothing changed with my son, but I was kind of dazed & sleepy and didn't really care. haha

(Next is my favorite suggestion from a mom about making shorter goals ~ Marlane)

I was always wondering why a child isn't getting ready fast enough even when the plan is to go some place he really wants to go to like the playground or a party. Then I realized that he just can't see the whole picture. I guess they live so much and intensely into the moment, now, that what will happen 15 minutes later just doesn't matter.
So I decided to make shorter goals let's say and it works for us in most cases. So instead of saying get ready to go to some place, I say things like: when you get ready would you like to open the door all by yourself? When you are ready would you like to get the lift?
For some reason they feel that these are very important jobs to do for strong big boys so they really want to do them
It works even better when there are two kids competing with each other who is going to do it first.
Another thing that they like is getting a small vitamin D out of the box and taking it all by themselves so I use that as well. (When you get ready would you like to take the vitamin D all by yourself?)
There was a time when they were getting another vitamin like a gummy bear and they were getting dressed so fast in order to open the

box and get the vitamin all by themselves.

In other words I give a reason why they should get dressed which feels like a privilege for them to do all by themselves. It motivates them to get moving. Because the bigger plan even if it's for their own pleasure they just don't get it always.

Oh and we also race in several occasions when we need to move faster. The dialogue is: ok I'm Mc queen and you are Miguel (from cars). Let's see who is going to put first socks on etc. We play different steam engines or other vehicles as well... The race thing has never failed me. Or we play the same thing to *kita*.

* (Marlane Wingo) My response = Thanks so much for taking the time to write this and share! UNBELIEVABLE! I can not believe this worked this morning. I followed your advice and simply told my son, hurry and put on your boots and jacket so you can open the front door by yourself. Are you kidding me?! We were out in 20 seconds flat.

WE'RE NOT ALL IN THE SAME BOAT - BANKSY

In comparing products, ideas, concerns and parenting techniques - no matter how big or small, or of importance - parents all over the world might not be in the same boat, but we are all trying to reach the same destination. We want our children to be happy. We want our children to have more of whatever we had less of as a child.

One day at Alec's German *kita*, the children had their first field trip. They were going to the zoo. The age range was from one and a half to three years old. Alec was one of the youngest at the time. Although the zoo was near, they still had to take a public bus to get there. I was instantly nervous and excited when I found out about the trip - definitely more nervous than excited, but I wasn't the only one.

The day came when ten toddlers arrived with their ten new backpacks and ten moms clutching their hands. The ten moms that would not leave the *kita* until the ten children were completely out of sight. The ten moms that nervously hung around another fifteen minutes discussing the joy and pain of watching our little ones grow up too fast. The ten moms representing six different countries: Germany, Peru, Turkey, Guinea, Portugal and America. We all had a different journey, but we arrived.

Every country's path to this destination is not cookie cutter. Our cultural traits make up the differences. It's sometimes difficult to understand our differences, but we can still respect our desire to get to the same destination. We all share a common goal. Let's work together and contribute whatever resources we have to share. Think of how many beautiful stories we will create.

Passports

MY BIRTHDAY SUIT

The stereotype is true. Europeans love being naked; more accurately, the Germans. I thought the French did as well, but they're all talk. Besides, I can't take the French seriously about optional clothing since they banned the burkini; quickly overturned a few days later due to social media outcry.

I consider myself a pretty open-minded individual, and this topic is no exception. But a real life experience of taking it all off in public is not the everyday norm as an American. I possess enough confidence to get down to my bikini bottoms. In the U.S., I had been to two clothing optional beaches: Little Beach in Makena, Maui, Hawaii and a small section of Fire Island, New York (nudity has now been banned by New York state law).

In Europe, I have only been to a handful of nudist beaches. In orthodox christian Greece, there is the world famous island of

Mykonos that has plenty of nude beaches for both gay and straight. More than ten years ago, I went to Super Paradise Beach. The right side was gay and the left side was Italian sunbathers. One doesn't need to draw a line in the sand. The gay side was…well, gay. And the Italian side was a Versace commercial. It swarmed with topless women in black bikini bottoms and men in black, square-cut, speedos. The Italians tinseled in gold jewelry while the other side wore their glitter in conversation and music.

But nothing could prepare me for the nude fest in Germany. My first very close encounter(s) was at my local gym - more like an upscale amusement park for adults. It has an indoor climbing wall, saunas (indoor and outdoor), steam room, swimming pool, whirlpools, meditation/relaxation lounge, restaurant, health/juice bar and a Koi fish pond surrounded by a sunbathing area. Even the gym floor is carpeted! I didn't want to join because it's the kind of gym where you already have to be skinny to go work out. And to my later realization: you had to be a nudist a.k.a. German.

Jens and I received a full tour of the gym/spa by a sales person before joining. With the exception of places you wear gym shoes, everyone is frolicking around in their birthday suit. And it is completely co-ed besides the locker rooms. In addition to showers in the locker rooms, there are also showers in the co-ed area in the case you want to rinse off with the opposite sex. I quickly asked the sales person if I could at least wear a bikini in these nude-friendly areas. I received a direct German answer, "Yes, but people will stare at you." Kind of the opposite effect, huh? After this reassurance, I became a member.

Before we had Alec, Jens and I used to frequent there together. It's an enjoyable couple activity. The first time we went, it was a glorious

summer day. We were in agreement to go layout by the pond. It was
packed; full of flesh, pure nakedness. At the time, I was about four
months pregnant and had a slight bump. I was already screaming
inside of self-conscious issues. Not of being pregnant with a few extra
pounds but simply thinking I was going to have to undress in front of a
jam packed crowd.

We found two lounge chairs and squeezed in with the other
sardines. Jens was naked lickety-split. *Oh, god.* I took my sweet time
preparing myself for the whole ordeal. *Oh, god.* I put the sunscreen on
way too fast. *Oh, god.* I came to the conclusion that I should lather on
a top-coat to take up more time. Jens noticed my deliberation. *Oh, god.*

"What are you doing?" Jens.

"Just putting on some extra sunscreen," me.

"Would you just relax," Jens.

"I am relaxed. I just think I should put more sunscreen on," me.

"Why" Jens.

"Because I'm pregnant," me.

"Hmmm…" Jens.

"Hey, what if we run into one of our neighbors here?" me.

"Yeah…And?" Jens.

"Wouldn't you feel a little uneasy or weird?" me.

"No, why should I?" Jens.

"Uuuummm…because you're naked," me.

"Nope," Jens.

"Really? Come on…what if one of your co-workers saw you?" me.

"Oh, sweetie, the world will keep turning," Jens.

Again, what a German I married. I laid there frozen in the sun for a
total of four minutes and took off. I am all for culture, but I wasn't
feeling it. I vowed not to return until I had Alec, and my boobs had

returned to their normal non-pornographic size.

However, I did return to the gym/spa but with my dependable bikini bottoms. And it was sensational! For a woman, swimming in a pool without a top should be a constitutional right; you and the water. No elastic to fight. Smooth lines. A dolphin. Ok, maybe completely nude would be like a dolphin, but my bottoms were staying put.

Even with all the other gym members showing their schnitzels and sausages, I was definitely getting some looks. But I didn't mind. I felt great in my lycra fabric until the sauna clothing police caught up with me.

"Blah, blah, blah, blah (some German that I didn't understand)," male gym employee.

"Do you speak English?" me.

"Of course," gym employee.

I always get this response.

"You can not wear those," he said, pointing to my trusty bikini bottom.

"Oh, yes I can. I was told by the sales representative that I could wear them," me confidently.

I have discovered that many Germans don't know the word representative in English, and I wanted to throw him off. Being stripped down to a small piece of clothing that is not big enough to blow my nose on, I am usually on high alert and ready for the most embarrassing moment in my life to occur.

"No, you can not wear them in the sauna. The sales representative was incorrect," gym employee.

Damn it! He knows the word representative.

"Why not? What's the big deal?" me.

"For hygiene reasons, you can not wear any clothing in the sauna," gym employee.

Why was this guy bothering me about a four by four square inch piece of spandex when we were all lugging around a huge two meter beach towel?! In the dry saunas, one must lay or sit on a towel.

There I was practically stark naked arguing with a guy who is wearing an entire outfit. I realized two things: I had officially earned the most stares, and I was going to have to remove my bikini bottom. I acknowledged my defeat and humiliatingly slid them off in front of the gym guy; who, of course, was good looking.

BABIES IN THEIR BIRTHDAY SUITS

Naturally, the Germans don't mind that their babies get naked, too. Their little nude colonies are mostly at beaches and swimming pools. And what's cuter than a naked baby? Two naked babies? A kitten? I can't think of anything else.

We have two beautiful, free, public, kiddie pools that are in nearby parks that we love to take Alec. One pool size is about thirty by fifty feet, and the water is only one foot deep. The other is a slow gradual depth from a few inches to one foot. They are not typical swimming pools like in the States where there is a mass amount of concrete and vending machines. There is lush grass that tip-toes up to the pools' edge; entirely hugged by nature. And in this nature are naked babies and toddlers. Since Hamburg is limited to its warm sunny days, many parents go there for their children to soak up the rich Vitamin D.

But there's an exception with naked babies that makes me a bit standoffish: PEKiP - *Prager Eltern-Kind-Programm* (Prague parent-child program). It's a baby course to help develop their sensory skills and time to bond with their parents. But it's done entirely naked - not the parents - the babies. Diapers are not be worn in the class. As you can imagine, pee and poo are an issue. There are plastic/rubber mats covering the floor for easier cleanup. Each class can have up to ten babies. So one must be careful where they step. I gross out with Alec's poo so, I certainly don't want to see or smell another baby's.

What I do appreciate are clothed classes for moms and babies/ toddler. My *hebamme* gave a postpartum stretch/exercise class - paid for by the lovely German government - back at our local community center. Alec and I participated with seven other moms and their little darlings.

Also, I had been searching and asking around for toddler yoga classes but have only found them starting at the age of three. Instead of being crazy and proactive, I decided not to start a yoga course for younger children. Me being a children's soccer coach is enough.

I am not a yoga person, but sometimes I will bust out my yoga mat and do a few moves. Alec gleefully joins in. After seeing his excitement and downward-dog, I googled yoga positions for toddlers. We even end with prayer hands and a *namaste*.

COFFEE BREAK

Let's shift gears and years - and travel to Spain. One of my all time favorite cultural mishaps, which proved to be a great life lesson, is my Spanish coffee story.

I was in Madrid for a month in 2002 just for a short stint. On my third day, I already was dating a Spanish guy.

I rented a small furnished apartment and lived amongst the locals. My kitchen wasn't fully equipped with appliances, and I had to stake out a place to get my morning coffee. On my corner, there was a small café. In my best broken Spanish, I ordered a coffee-to-go. They brought me a coffee but in a cup with a saucer.

"Ummm…excuse me. I'm really, really sorry but I wanted a coffee-to-go."

After much confusion in English and Spanish, I gulped down my coffee while standing up at the counter and left. The next morning, before heading out the door, I quickly looked up how to say "coffee-to-go, please" in my Spanish book. I hesitated before going in again, but it was the only place I could get coffee before the subway and directly on my corner. This was my coffee-fix corner, and I was going to do it! Thought the overly enthusiastic American go-getter.

"Coffee, please. To-go, please. Coffee-to-go, please." (Me dumbly speaking slow Spanish.)

Surely, they would get it right this time. Nope. I must have repeated those words ten times before someone came up and explained that they only serve coffee sitting down. I glanced around. It wasn't some hipster or fancy place with wait service. But my puzzled, distraught face got me a coffee in a waxy, plastic Coca-Cola cup. Anticipating my next request, the guy stacked another cup underneath. I didn't know these cups still existed. I spoke to my Spanish *quase* boyfriend about what went down.

"You what?" asked Sergio.

"Yeah, it was hilarious. I ordered a coffee-to-go, and they brought me a coffee in these old fashioned waxy Coca-Cola cups. You know, for fountain drinks," I said, laughing.

"But you can't order a coffee-to-go," Sergio.

"What are you talking about? I can order a coffee-to-go."

"Oh my god. You are so American," Sergio.

"What's American about it?"

"In Spain, you don't order coffee-to-go. You sit down and drink your coffee," Sergio.

"I don't understand," unapologetically.

"No one gets their coffee-to-go!" proclaimed Sergio.

"This is Madrid not a small village," I said, not letting it go.

"Yeah, it doesn't matter (then some mumbling in Spanish)," Sergio.

I continued to argue with Señor Sergio until I got bored from going in circles. But a few days later, it struck me. It's not part of the Spanish culture to hurry with food and dining. I mean, what other country takes a two-hour lunch? I don't know which is worse: the Spanish siesta or Germany's rule on Sunday where everything is closed. I mean everything: supermarkets, banks, pet stores, shopping malls. Closed. Lockdown.

Of course that was back in 2002 and now one can get a takeaway coffee not only at coffee shop chains but many Spanish cafés, too. And served in a paper cup with a recycled cup sleeve and a plastic lid that says "caution hot contents!" Any special requests? No problem! We got you covered: fat free, sugar free, soy, extra foam, shots, syrup, extra hot; however, there is one request that still might make an European barista squirm: decaf.

Now, a bit older and wiser, I feel nostalgic for the white cup and saucer that brings a short intermission during our hurried day and a conversation with a happy-outlook-on-life waiter. Or merely I produce a smile that says, *I want to sit here and not talk to anyone and drink my coffee in peace.*

And to my surprise or not, guess what Sergio is doing twelve years later? Selling coffee in Dubai along with international dishes in his incredibly successful restaurants and cafés. He is more than happy to serve you a coffee-to-go, but secretly, he prefers you to sit and slow down.

TODDLER SOCCER

There are two common cultural traits shared in the world: soccer and coffee. I started playing soccer when I was five years old. Alec started when he was eighteen months old, and I am his coach! I may not be the quintessential French woman, but I am THE soccer mom in Hamburg.

It was an unspoken fact soccer would be a part of Alec's life. Jens and I both played soccer and still try to when time and our aging bodies allow it. My two older brothers played as well, sharing the same jersey number twelve. Our father was often our coach growing up, and he coached our high school soccer teams.

Jens even has a soccer sports star in his family Norbert Nigbur (his father's cousin). He was a goalkeeper on the West German National team winning the World Cup in 1974. Norbert played hundreds of games in the *Bundesliga* (German Soccer League); most famously known from playing with FC Schalke.

I have imagined going to Alec's soccer games and watching him play. But I never anticipated to be Alec's coach and especially never so early! How it came to be was from the World Cup 2014.

All three of us had watched a few world cup games. Alec was having fun pointing at the ball on TV and was very interested in his father's excitement. I was totally pumped from the games and Alec's enthusiasm. It made me jump on the computer to search for a local children's soccer group; except there weren't any. I couldn't believe it. We live in Germany's second largest city, and there were no kids soccer leagues or classes to be found; only starting with four years of age.

Coincidentally, a mother posted in an expat Facebook group asking about toddler soccer programs in Hamburg. Through a long thread of comments from many other moms inquiring about the same thing and "following" as to receive a name of a soccer league/club, I realized there was no organization catering to this age group.

I gave it about a week's thought, and decided I would organize and coach a soccer class or two for Alec. If it turned into a complete disaster with coaching such a young group, it would make for some very entertaining material for the book. Also, it would be a good opportunity to become active in this Hamburg mothers group. Moms schedule play dates, give baby/child and expat advice, and a ton of other great information about raising a child. And Facebook language specific groups are a great resource for helping your child learn another language. For example, finding events/activities in a target language and native speaking babysitters.

Shortly thereafter, I posted on the same meet-up group that I was hosting a free soccer class from twelve months to under three years. It was on a Saturday morning for forty-five minutes in a public park. Fourteen children showed up, and I was the only coach! Go! Luckily, I had requested beforehand that the parents stay and help their child since they are so young. With fourteen children and their parents, the class was enormous. But somehow I managed and received a lot of praises. It encouraged me to do another and another. I even had a class in a different part of Hamburg and started my own Facebook group with ninety-three members and counting!

One rainy Saturday morning, I had to cancel soccer practice. I posted on Facebook, "Soccer is canceled. If you are British…Football is cancelled." I thought I was pretty savvy until a friend messaged me and said, "You'd better add fußball as well." This is when it first hit me: We are a global family. I quickly posted and added fußball for the German crowd.

It's a relief to have a morning activity for Alec on the weekends. It gets us moving and out of the house. And of course we all get to participate. Since I'm coaching, Jens has to help Alec with the exercises and drills. While I am an airplane flying around a tree with fourteen children riding my tail, Jens is busy helping Alec be a pilot, too. Coaching toddlers is like herding a bunch of cats or in my warm-up exercise, being an air traffic controller.

But the reward of forty-five minutes of pure chaos is worth it. They look at you as if you are Santa Claus. All the wonder and excitement in their faces is a thousand butterfly kisses. I want to stop soccer practice and squeeze each and everyone of their cutie pie cheeks and tell them what a great job they are doing. The joy of teaching these adorable creatures makes me selfishly continue.

Our soccer practices are not hard core training sessions. It's basically singing and rhyme-time with a soccer ball. Oh, and dancing; lots of dancing. We also waddle like penguins, swim like the polar bears, stomp like elephants and hop like kangaroos. My favorite though is when we sing "If You're Happy and You Know It!" I channel Mr. Kanamori's happiness philosophy and implement it anytime possible. Another grateful, feel good song is "Happiness is Something if you Give it Away."

SOCCER VS FUSSBALL

After one soccer class, a mom of a four-year-old boy told me how much she appreciated that I taught soccer in a fun way with songs and a lot of encouragement. She went on to explain that her son was in a soccer program and her child was cut after a few training sessions. Cut! He was four! She had a conversation with the coach about why he was let go and couldn't understand why everything was taken so seriously at this age. She asked, "I thought soccer was supposed to be fun?" The coach replied, "Soccer isn't fun." Eek!

We do believe in structured learning for Alec but don't want to suck the joy out of the experience. Jens said that he wants Alec to enjoy soccer like everything else in life so, that Alec will want to keep returning to it. We also try to apply this train of thought to education and learning languages. At this age, learning by playing is by far one of the greatest methods.

After a couple of rainy Saturday mornings, I started searching for indoor spaces and soccer fields to hold the classes. There aren't any fields in Hamburg that are available to the public. Instead there are proper soccer clubs that own fields and some have indoor activity centers for their members; most are attached with a bar and restaurant as well.

I visited one club near my home to inquire about offering a class for young children. Their club has a class once a week for three to five year olds. Any child can join in for ten euro per month.

I had a scheduled meeting with the head organizer and prepared myself for the discussion but slight problem. He could only meet during the week at 4pm. I ended up bringing Alec to a somewhat of a business meeting. This is when I witnessed Alec as a young gentleman. During the meeting, he sat next to me, busy playing with his truck and sipping his water: no loud outbursts and no chasing him around the room. It lasted for thirty minutes! I could get use to this.

A friend of mine has had her boys on a waiting list for fifteen months at another soccer club and still no word. I asked the soccer organizer at the meeting if they had a waiting list.

"No, we don't have a waiting list," organizer.

"Great! I'll tell my friend about your club," me.

"No. We don't have any spaces," organizer.

"Well, how does one get on a team?" me.

"You can't get on a team, but there is a possibility," organizer.

"Well, which age group do you have space available?" me.

"None at the moment, but there is a possibility," organizer.

Huh? I was so confused. I felt like I was having a conversation with a master negotiator. The kind where you ask a simple question or want a direct response to a problem and all they say is *I understand what you are saying* and skirt around the issue. This guy's phrase was *it's a possibility*. What a open ended phrase! Neither a yes or no. I shared it with Jens later that evening in order for him to use it at work.

"I'm sorry. I don't understand. So how is it possible to get on a team?" Relentless me, that can never let anything go.

"Well, you have to talk to the coach. Each child is different," organizer.

It finally clicked. I'm so slow sometimes! I realized how exclusive and elite soccer can be even for children in Hamburg and perhaps the rest of Germany. Not in the sense that only wealthy children can be a part of soccer but only the talented. The three to under five-year-old classes the clubs host are only a front to scout out the good players. Then when they turn five, the skilled players have a spot on the team, and the rest are cut. That's where the fun ends. Even as young as five years of age, having a place on a team is coveted.

So what happens to the kids that are five years old and were not invited to play in the club but want to keep playing soccer? Bad news. There are scarcely any soccer classes and no team games. Pretty sad, huh? I did find a couple of alternatives; a couple of gyms that offer soccer classes for kids starting with five years old, but in addition to the soccer class fee, one has to pay for a full membership to the gym.

There are also body movement courses for young children that get them excited about sports but not related to soccer specifically.

I grew up in a small Texas town when it was roughly 16,000 people, and I played in a soccer association where anyone could play soccer no matter what their skill level. No one was turned away. The age range was five to fifteen years. Then one would play on their high school team. My parents reminded me that "back in the day" they paid about twenty dollars per season (fall/spring). That bought a jersey, matching socks, and fees to cover the cost of referees. That twenty dollars also bought an opportunity to have some pure, honest, good-hearted fun.

MAMA'S GET-AWAY

Another inspiration from soccer - again the World Cup 2014 - was (is) traveling. After watching a world cup game on a Sunday evening, I declared to Jens, "I have lived in Europe for two years and haven't gone anywhere!" While that statement isn't exactly true, we have been many places in Germany and once to Spain. But watching all these international teams play and thinking about all the countries, I got anxious about traveling.

"Well, then go," Jens replied.

"Yeah, but we have Alec, and it's difficult to travel with him. I want to visit some cities. See the sites and museums."

"So *you* just go," Jens.

"What? Really? Just me?"

"Yes, I can stay here with him," Jens.

Jens had a couple weeks vacation coming up, and he suggested that I take a few days and go somewhere. Within a couple of hours, I booked all my flights and hotels lickity split. No way I was going to let too much time pass so, he could re-think his offer.

Alec was eighteen months old when I went on my get-away. It was the first time I was apart from him; four nights. But we Skyped every day, and I told him about my traveling adventures.

I strongly recommend this to any new parent to take some time and get away. I flew to Helsinki and Copenhagen. Remarkable how close they are to Hamburg, but the Scandinavian countries are so different!

Not having Alec motivated me to travel light. I can't believe I only took a backpack. No checked baggage is pure freedom. Ironic how stuff weighs you down. In a cruel way, one of the best things about my trip was witnessing parents struggle with the diaper bag, stroller wheels getting stuck, screaming children, flying pacifiers, milk bottles landing on the floor and a hodgepodge of other necessary objects parents must bring when leaving the house even for a short walk around the block.

In the future, we will travel with Alec a great deal. But for now it's not the right time for exploring cities and meandering museums with a baby or toddler. My advice is to stick to child friendly resorts and beaches.

THE LOVE OF SOCCER

Soccer has continuously inspired and transformed me. Even with the crisis in Syria, I found a way to help through soccer. My heart ached in sorrow as I continuously heard about the horrific war tragedies happening in Syria. How could we watch another one die?

The burning image of the young boy washed up on the shore was too much for me. I couldn't shake the picture of him laying face down in the sand. That little boy deserved more. He deserved more than dying at the age of three. And so did the other four children that drowned with him.

I had to do something. What could I do? The refugees needed humanitarian assistance. They needed a way out. It was time for civic participation. At the time, Germany was helping with the displaced Syrian refugees. Many were coming to Hamburg and neighboring cities. This was it! This was the time for me to do something! Something to ease my selfish pain.

I donated money. I donated clothing and food. Once I drove to greet them at a train station and handed out water bottles with a friend. I witnessed the tired bodies pass by and locked eyes with bloodshot red-eyes.

I wanted all those images to go away. It hurt; a real nightmare. The worst is when I replace Alec with a refugee child in my head.

Around the time of the 9/11 anniversary in 2015, a friend posted a video on Facebook called *Boatlift, An Untold Tale of 9/11 Resilience* narrated by Tom Hanks. I never knew that 500,000 people were transported to safety on September 11th via boats but not just public boats; private boats, too. Boat owners volunteered and courageously helped bring a half a million people to safe shores, away from danger. These brave folks stepped up and did the right thing. In the video, a beautiful quote, "everyone has a little bit of hero in them…it will come out when you are needed." And as the historian Fritz Stern encourages, "individual acts of decency and courage make a difference." [1]

This is how I got the idea to do a soccer fundraiser for the Syrian refugees. I thought what specific thing can I contribute to help? I drew a blank. How was I going to approach this situation? I didn't know their culture. I didn't know these people. How was I to help if I didn't know them? But it finally came to me: soccer. It's a fun, positive cultural identity we all share. Everyone knows soccer, and it's something I know very well.

I thought donating soccer balls would be a way to connect with the refugees; to be given something familiar. It's incredibly difficult to be in unfamiliar lands not knowing the language or culture. Everything is confusing and different. But one thing remains the same: the love of the sport, the love of soccer.

So, I hosted a kid's soccer practice fundraiser and raised donations to purchase soccer balls. As I handed over the balls at the refugee donation center, my pain eased. I was humbled. I was grateful to help. I was also grateful not to be on the receiving end.

No one has all the answers and solutions. But devastation from war and human disaster can not be ignored. Showing compassion is what it means to be human. And we show compassion by treating others how we would want to be treated. Friends, there is a name for it: equality.

A few days later, I was jogging around our neighborhood. This particular jog included a pit-stop for a ham and cheese croissant. My friend Whitney calls this a French marathon. I decided to walk and glutinously stuff my face at the same time to counter act a few calories when I saw some huge stacked storage containers. I had never noticed them before because they are set back a ways from the road and surrounded by trees. Thinking we could use some storage for all of our excessively accumulated stuff, I walked over to get some information and a security guard stopped me. Wow, they have high fencing and security, I thought. This is going to be too far out of our budget.

"*Kann ich Ihnen helfen?*" (Can I help you?) asked the guard.

"*Können Sie bitte English sprechen?*" (Can you please speak English?) asked the lazy American mom.

"Of course! I have sailed for more than thirty years all over the world!" piped up the guard.

Mental "yes" and fist pump thrown in the air.

"What is this place?" I asked, noticing a small playground and recycling containers.

"It's a place for asylum-seekers," he answered.

"People live here? In these metal containers?!" I asked with a bewildered face. "Is it for the Syrian refugees?"

"Yes and others," he said.

I'm not sure how long I stood there in silence, but the guard let me soak it all in. I hadn't been prepared for his answer. With tears in my eyes, I thanked him for his help. Before walking away, I noticed inside a small front office some volleyballs and soccer balls on a top shelf.

"Do they play soccer here?" I inquired.

"Sure they do!" he happily answered.

"Can I bring some balls here?" I asked.

The guard patiently explained that they probably had enough, but he told me the proper procedure of donating items so other centers might receive them, too.

The next time I passed by the containers, I was in the car with Alec. I slowed down and stretched my neck to see what my neighbors were up to. There were a few guys playing soccer. I looked into the rear view mirror and said, "I love you, Alec." I pumped up the music and sped away.

Written on the Berlin Wall, "Many small people, who in many small places, do many small things, can alter the face of the world."

OMRAN

Today is August 19, 2016. Another image burning appears that will also haunt me. The video of the little boy - Omran. The CNN video showed Omran being carried into an ambulance with blood seeping from his head down his gray dust colored face. He sheds no tears, but I cried my eyes out.

Today is September 11, 2016. I held another kid's soccer practice fundraiser for the refugees and asylum seekers in Hamburg. We were supposed to have it a week earlier, but it got rained out. I rescheduled it to the next Sunday not realizing at the time it would be 9/11. It's always an eerie, sad day for me. But we ended up having a fun time, and it felt more special. It's almost been exactly a year since the last fundraiser, and my thoughts turn to the Syrian people and the war… *has anything changed?*

A POEM

Politically Correct in a Politically Incorrect World

I watch the refugees walking through the subway corridor.
Your Flatiron building face and the blistering-red earthquake fault
lines in your eyes pierce my compassion.
I motion you to take the coat from my arms.
You direct your son to take it.
I'm sorry the lining is fluorescent pink. But it's ok…there are no gender colors here.
I hand you a bottle of Nestlé water.
I'm sorry it is Nestlé. It was the only water at the drugstore.
Wherever you end up, I want you to know that I think about you and your son.
Do something…your aura engulfs me.
Do something.

~ Marlane Wingo

⁂ Bonus Chapter 7

Cross-border Collaboration

U.S. DAYCARE VERSUS THE GERMAN *KITA*

In Hamburg, everyone receives FREE daycare. My fellow Americans, do I have your attention? In the U.S., "…child care was parents' biggest annual expense, averaging about $12,500 a year nationwide." [1] Many American families seek help from grandparents or mothers give up their careers and take care of the children.

When a child turns one years old in Germany, parents receive a humongous discount on daycare depending on their salary. The German government subsidizes by roughly paying 85% of the cost. And, in Hamburg, daycare is entirely free up to twenty-five hours per week. Additionally, if more hours are needed because of work, attending university or a work program, it's free. For example, when I attended German language classes, I received additional daycare hours. We pay nothing for daycare! Zero! Yes, taxes are higher in Germany, but one receives more social services and everyone benefits.

More importantly than cost, German daycares are run by qualified caregivers. In the U.S., "Only a high school degree or an equivalent-earned online is necessary..." [2] In Germany, a caregiver must take a two year program through a university, and to be a leader of a group (7 to 14 children), one needs a three year childcare degree. [3] Sometimes heavy government regulation is a good thing because who knows who is taking care of your child? I can assure you the German government does.

In America, daycare laws vary greatly depending on the state. Many states do not require child caregivers to be licensed or even perform a criminal background check. [4] A persuasive reason for the U.S. to have government-supplied daycare: to protect the safety of the children.

"In the long run, it's probably self-financing. The kids who grow up 10 to 20 years from now would be more likely to earn higher wages and avoid contact with the criminal justice system," said Josh Bivens, research and policy director at the Economic Policy Institute. [5]

But who wants to work at a daycare in the U.S. when they make an average of $10.31 per hour? [6] In order to achieve the success that Bivens is speaking of, all countries must provide qualified daycare providers. And governments are only going to get qualified workers by offering an enticing wage; at the very least, a living wage. We should treat our caregivers, including elderly caregivers, with as much respect and compensation they deserve. Anne-Marie Slaughter, author of *Unfinished Business*, explains, "Caring for children properly, and valuing the unpaid and paid work of those who undertake this vital job, will determine America's future competitiveness, security, equality, and the wellbeing of its citizens. And at the other end of life, who are we if we do not care for those who cared for us?" [7]

WORKING FAMILIES IN THE UNITED STATES

Women and men (in all countries) should demand high-quality, affordable childcare, pre-kindergarten programs, and after-school activities for all. [8]

The good ol' U.S.A. was shamed in 2015 when the United Nations sent three foreign women to the U.S. to assess gender equality. The delegates "found the U.S. to be lagging far behind international human rights standards" such as "its 23 percent gender pay gap, maternity leave, affordable child care and treatment of female migrants in detention centers."

But what the most shocking thing the delegates discovered is exactly what prompted me to write this chapter. "Perhaps the biggest surprise of their trip was learning that women in the country (U.S.) don't seem to know what they're missing." [9] Frances Raday, human rights expert, said some American women didn't know that in other countries mothers had paid maternity leave. All developed countries, except the U.S., offer paid leave.

The Project on Global Working Families conducted a report from 177 countries and found that only five nations do not guarantee paid leave for mothers: Lesotho, Liberia, Papua New Guinea, Swaziland and the U.S. This is not a trait shared by the Free World.

In the seventies, the women's movement in United States of America was a huge success. Equality was starting to be recognized in the workforce, and the Equal Rights Amendment - even though it didn't pass into law - helped give women the confidence to question traditional gender roles. Think of the mother in Leave it to Beaver: moms are homemakers, and their decisions are only to be made in the kitchen. Also, before the movement, college was encouraged more to young men. This result of cultural conditioning in the States had worked for a very long time, but outspoken, radical women led the push forward.

But what failed with the movement is that America didn't implement an infrastructure to support working families. It was an all-or-nothing approach. Moms wanted to work but also wanted to be moms. But the American government didn't play fairly. They basically said, "If you want to work, great. That's fine with us. But we are not going to promote or encourage women to work." Women finally given the ok to work, but no programs or laws were in place to let them be a *working mom*.

For example, what happens when a child gets sick and has to stay home from school or daycare? More than likely, mom has to take off work. A lot of U.S. companies - by law - don't have to give paid sick days. Zero. What are parents supposed to do when a company's policy for maternity leave is only for a two weeks? Or none at all? Many times, the mother quits her job because daycare would cost more than her paycheck. What happens when the father has a more demanding, higher paying job than the mother? The mother gives up her career to stay at home to raise the children or takes a humdrum, mindless part-time job to fit the children's schedule. She becomes the primary caregiver.

A mother's career is often completely over when entering back into the workforce. She is usually met with a lower paying and lower stimulating job. She wants her career back, not for it to be replaced with a job. This type of woman may not suffer as a housewife from *The Feminine Mystique* - "a vague undefined wish for 'something more' than washing dishes, ironing, punishing and praising the children". [10] But couldn't a woman with a mindless job suffer for 'something more'? People can feel empty with housework as well as in a boring job and crave "the need for self-fulfillment". [11, 12]

FOR THE WOMAN WHO WANTS IT ALL

Anne-Marie Slaughter, past director of policy planning for the U.S. State Department (and dean of Princeton's Woodrow Wilson School or Public and International affairs), stated in an interview regarding working mothers, "I still strongly believe that women can 'have it all'…But not today, not with the way America's economy and society are currently structured." Her phrase "having it all" refers to women who want a career and to be an active/engaged parent. Slaughter strongly suggests that companies should make it possible for women to make their own hours. The kind of flexibility to balance work and family life the way they want to. If not, the result will be that companies will continue to lose talent. [13]

This is how the economy suffers, too. The workforce loses skilled, specialized labor due to women moving into undemanding jobs. Obviously, another untapped resource are full-time housewives. Yes, there is always the possibility to re-invent oneself *if* you have the time and money. The burden of raising a child in America, simply weighs more on a woman because there is a gigantic void in laws to support working moms/working families.

Now let's talk about unspoken cultural truths in America. In 2004, the U.S. Department of Labor held a survey to confirm that "the average working woman spends about twice as much time as the average working man on household chores and the care of children." [14] So on top of struggling at work with few federal laws to protect their motherhood, women contribute more time on chores and children - of course unpaid.

"Ensuring equality on the home front" is just as important as in the work place. [15] Women should be equal in all realms of society. Could this be the reason why there is such a pay gap? Because women's work in the house goes unpaid? A mentality that women do work for free - the cooking, cleaning, being the primary caregiver for the children and elderly. Not to mention the overwhelming amount of emotional labor/work given to the children. I would rather do ten piles of laundry than suffer from the stress of being a full-time therapist to my toddler. The demands, tantrums, constant negotiating, crying is exhausting and consumes so much time and energy.

Before women even look for a job, we have been determined as free, unpaid help. Is this the reason why women are inferior to men in pay? Because of the stigma of unpaid work and care in the home? Could this also be the reason why women have such a difficult time asking for a raise? Because we believe we are not worthy since we are used to doing work for free? That we should just be happy and grateful to even have a job. That is fear. That is not knowing your worth. That is not believing in yourself. And that's exactly what a company wants you to believe. They want you to feel inferior and not know your worth.

COMPANY VERSUS FAMILY

On average, French women go back to work from maternity leave anytime from six weeks to six months. Americans start as early as one or two weeks depending on their company and which state they reside. Also, it might be unpaid leave. Unbelievable! A company's interest is protected while mothers and fathers do not get to stay home with their newborn babies.

I have a relative living in Texas that initially received only two weeks of maternity leave from her boss. She ended up having a C-section so, her boss gave her an extra week. *How gracious of her* - with an inexplicable amount of sarcasm. FYI, her boss is a mother!

By law, U.S. companies that have fifty employees or less don't have to offer any maternity leave! What does this say about how we treat our families?

I will say it again: In all 50 states, if a private sector company has 50 employees or less, it does not have to allow *any* unpaid time off. [16, 17] What does this say about how the UNITED STATES OF AMERICA treats their citizens? Is this America's idea of family values? Is this freedom?

"The UK guarantees 40 weeks. Canada offers 17 weeks. Ireland provides 26 weeks. Mexico offers 12 weeks. Japan guarantees 14 weeks. Even Bangladesh, a country criticized for poor worker treatment, offers 16 weeks' leave. In fact, the U.S. is still the only highly developed country in the world that doesn't offer federal paid maternity leave." [18]

In addition, expecting moms in the U.S. do not receive any time off before the birth unless the company grants it. It's common for a woman's water to break at work! In Germany, all women are not allowed by law to work *six weeks* before the due date and receive unemployment pay/benefits.

I was overjoyed when Mark Zuckerberg of Facebook announced he would be giving four months parental leave to his employees. This benefit came shortly after he became a new dad; before it was two months. For the most part, management dictates family leave across the U.S. And speaking of Facebook, Sheryl Sandberg wrote a post describing how single parenting is incredibly difficult in the U.S. Her husband passed a year before. She even went as far to say, "We need to rethink our public and corporate workforce policies and broaden our understanding of what a family is and looks like." [19] I think both Zuckerberg and Sandberg deserve a big "good job", but it's not enough. These two are heavy hitters in the U.S. - *excuse me* - in the world. Power players like these guys are the ones that need to swing their weight around and help bring laws into action.

So why should it be the government's job to put laws in place to protect women? Sure not every job has paid maternity leave, but it is the woman's decision to work there, correct? Let me explain what happens when a company dictates benefits. Work ethics soon become obsolete.

There are laws in place to protect humans against corporate greed. For example, The Fair Labor Standards Act of 1938 [20], placed heavy restrictions on child labor. Also, before The Act, companies could have their employees working an unlimited amount of hours. The Act put into place a national minimum wage to help end slave labor. The laws also included that workers should receive overtime pay.

In addition, there are many laws for safe working conditions. How would you feel working in a factory in Bangladesh? Laws are in place to protect their people from corporations. Companies want to make profits, and the first place it looks to cut costs are with its employees.

So, if a company can make its own benefit packages like maternity leave, do you think they will offer it? No. Why would they? It simply doesn't make financial sense. Why hire a young woman knowing that they soon could become pregnant and will have to take off work or quit completely? If it were up to the companies, there would be no labor laws because it costs them money. A company's duty and loyalty are only to its shareholders.

What happens when there is no maternity protection for women? Simply, a woman is devalued because men are sought after more. For example, the wage gap in the U.S. Women only make 78 cents for every dollar a male makes. "When racism is added to the mix, inequality worsens." [21] The wage gap shouldn't be called a gap; rather, a *canyon*. Pope Francis also weighed in on saying, "Why should it be taken for granted that women must earn less than men? The disparity is pure scandal." [22]

GAPS IN THE AMERICAN DREAM

And mothers have to deal with another "gap" termed: Mommy Gap or Mommy Wage Gap. [23] Being away from the work force for a few years with gaps on a resume does not look good. Simply being a mom is a stigma for being denied jobs or less pay. [24] "Men seldom suffer the same prejudice; fatherhood usually helps their careers, giving them cachet of stability." [25]

When a woman is devalued at work because of her gender, she is denied many opportunities; sometimes even to be born. China has a one child policy because of culture preferences - many girls get aborted. In addition to culture preferences, men receive higher pay and better jobs so, boys are preferred in order to take care of their parents and other relatives in need. [26] Also, in many middle eastern countries, where there are no retirement packages, a male offspring's duty is to provide for their elders. [27] In 2012, the World Bank reported that sex-selective abortions and female infanticide occur more often in India, China, many parts of Asia, and in some Caucasus countries. [28]

When we do not treat each other with equality, someone always loses. And as Noam Chomsky explains in the movie *Requiem for the*

185

American Dream: inequality is corrosive to democracy. So why do countries with few labor/parental laws (U.S.) and third world countries continue to keep having babies? Because to most Americans, the idea of "the pursuit of happiness" consists of having a family.

In developing countries, one can ask the same question: Why bring a child into this world while living in poverty? Because the love of a child is unmeasurable. Because sometimes from one's economic status and powerless state, having children is the only means of joy. Should we tell people living in poverty that they are absolutely selfish and cruel to bring children into this world? Should having a child only be a right only to the wealthy and privileged? Should we make *A Modest Proposal* as Jonathan Swift suggested?

Parents will do all means necessary to give their child more than what they had as a child. But like the American dream of prosperity and success through hard work is it still possible? With all the hard work, is there enough family time? With all the hard work, do the children truly know both their parents? With all the hard work, does a father or mother receive the promotion? With all the hard work, does the American dream of prosperity and "the pursuit of happiness" matter when it's not even achievable anymore because it's pre-determined by companies instead of the protection from their government?

WELCOME TO GERMANY ~ *WILLKOMMEN IN DEUTSCHLAND*

This is a list of German laws that helps women and men have the freedom to be parents and promotes the rights and status of women. Also, through German law, equal rights for same sex parents (almost).

- By law, the mom-to-be is not allowed to work six weeks before the due date and eight weeks after. Paid with full salary.
- When a baby turns one years old, heavily discounted daycare (it's free in Hamburg) for five hours a day, five times a week - ranging from 50 to 180 Euros per month. Additional free hours are given to parents who both work full time.
- An abundance of community centers offering free and low-cost children programs
- Free exercise course (eight classes) for post pregnancy
- Midwife care before and after labor - usually two to three months before and six to eight weeks after.
- Mother & Father = 1 1/2 years each paid maternity leave
- Mother & Father = 3 years each of parental leave (company may not fire employee). May work part-time.
- *Elterngeld* (parent money) paid for 1 year. Maximum of 1,800 Euro per month.
- *Kindergeld* (child's money) is 184 to 215 Euros per child (per year) until 18 years of age. And will continue until 25 years of age if the child attends college.
- Health insurance
- Labor unions
- For all German citizens and people with work permits: 6 weeks paid vacation, 8 public holidays, paid sick days up to 12 weeks and unemployment insurance

When it comes to geographical locations in Europe, I lean more towards the EU and the Nordic countries for raising a child. These governments have put together a better social structure for families versus the U.S. It allows parents to have more time with their children and still have the option to work. For the mom who wants to have it all, a career and motherhood, it's more attainable in Europe - *kind of.* There are major changes that need to be addressed. For example, the British pay some serious quid for childcare. Oh, hold on, they are headed out of the EU - never mind them.

PROBLEMS IN THE FATHERLAND

Surprisingly, with all these social benefits comes a few glitches in Germany. There is preferential tax treatment based on marital status. This means that a married couple can have lower taxes. The German government bases it on the person who earns less. Take a wild guess who usually earns less in Germany? Women. So, it makes sense for a mother to take a part-time job (or not work at all), and the father leads with a better career and salary. Here are a few facts to support my statement that women make less, and how it's apparent in the workplace in Germany:

- Gender pay gap: Women earn 21.6 percent less than men as of 2016. [29]
- Members of the DAX (a stock index that represents 30 major German companies trading on the Frankfurt stock exchange) introduced a voluntary goal of 30% female managers by 2015. [30] Unfortunately, it didn't happen. Chancellor Angela Merkel even admitted in 2016 that it didn't work. "But at some point there had been so many hollow promises that it was clear - this isn't working." [31] Merkel is referring to the voluntary quotas. In my opinion, not many companies are going to *voluntary* do anything for labor.
- The G7 is "among the worst performing regions, with just 22%

of senior roles occupied by women and 39% of companies with no women in senior roles. Two of the worst performing individual countries are Japan, with just 7% senior roles held by women, and Germany, with 15%." [32]

Another glitch, only in Bavaria (a Southern federal state in Germany), is that moms get paid to stay at home hindering them from returning to work. It's called *Betreuungsgeld*, "one of Chancellor Angela Merkel's pet projects". [33] Parents have the option of receiving 150 euro per month instead of taking their children (under three years of age) to daycare.

In our case, Jens works and makes enough money for me to stay at home and write. Of course writing this book is a painstakingly, slow process since I have another job. The boss' name being Alec. But I am grateful and fortunate to even have an opportunity to write. As author Virginia Woolf puts it, "a woman must have money and a room of her own if she is to write fiction." Woolf explains, in *A Room of One's Own,* only through financial freedom/economic independence, women are able to become writers.

And there is another powerful opposing force that interferes with many moms from going back to work full-time or even part-time in Germany. The stereotype of a *rabenmutter* (raven mother). The term comes from mother ravens pushing their babies out of the nest. They fall to the ground, and the process of survival begins. This label is for German moms who go back to work, not stay-at-home moms, and don't care about their children. The label is fading but not quick enough. Germany has a very traditional history of stay-at-home mothers. Where does it come from? How did it start? I was shocked to discover that "until 1977, Western German women had to get permission from their husbands to work." [34]

Until 2012, Germany did not offer discounted daycare. And free daycare only started August 2014 in Hamburg. The cost for daycare was comparable to the U.S. or the U.K.; therefore, many mothers stayed home to avoid paying this excruciating expense. Like other countries with high daycare costs, this hinders mothers from returning to work until their children go to school. This is a major reason why the work culture for women, especially moms, is still so backwards.

The government must make it more appealing and flexible for German women to return to work. Extending school hours and offering after school activities is a good place to start. [35] There is much talk in Germany of making school schedules the same as work schedules; however, the new *Ganztagschulreformen* are according to some experts a "fake" program. Schools can choose between mandatory full-time school programs (which go until 3 or 4pm and include actual teachers teaching for that time) and optional full-time programs, where the afternoon activities are not really school related and are outsourced, oftentimes to the cheapest providers.

NO MOTHER LEFT BEHIND

It's great that Germany is now providing low cost and free daycare in some cities. But what about the mothers and fathers who didn't benefit from the inexpensive daycare? Will they be forgotten? Are there any work/training programs for re-entering the work force? Allowance for attending university without the competition of younger students?

It is an incredible benefit that mothers may have up to three years off work, but one is not guaranteed the same job returning back to work. Also, in Germany, most traditional grammar schools end between 12:30 to 2:00pm. This makes it difficult to have a full-time job. Once again, mothers tend to fill poorly paid part-time jobs to accommodate their children's schedule. Not many people can work their way up the corporate ladder as a part-timer. Sadly, the mom gives up her full-time job along with her career and has to start all over again.

Germany is so progressive in many ways, but when it comes to the workforce, women are limited to certain positions and lower roles. And a mother's career progress is greatly hindered by taking one to three years off of maternity leave. Could this explain why the growth population rate is negative in Germany like in Japan? [36] There have been numerous studies concluding women do not want to procreate because they would not have the same opportunities at work like their male counterparts. But the absence of women in leadership at work is blinding. I may not work in the corporate world right now, but I experienced the void - of all places, an experience at the Hamburg International Airport!

When I flew to Helsinki, July 2014, my flight was at 9:00am with a layover in Stockholm. Of course on a Monday morning, there are mostly business travelers, but I couldn't believe the swarms of men everywhere! I was one of a few women at the airport. If someone wants to meet a man with a job, go hang out at an airport from Monday to Friday in the morning. Good grief, don't waste your time at the bars. This is better than any dating website. It's even better than online dating because you know for sure they have a job and what they truly look like.

It was shocking being completely surrounded by men at the Hamburg airport. As I pulled out my clear plastic containers of shampoo and body wash from my backpack, all the businessmen pulled out their laptops, iPads and the latest gadgets. Besides having to wear a head scarf, I could have easily been in Saudi Arabia.

Here's one thing that burns me about Germany in the work place. On one's *C.V.* (resume), it is common practice to put your age, marital status, number of children, sometimes religion and picture! If you do not wish to put this information, the hiring company can request it. By law, it is not discrimination. Good luck getting the job if you refuse to supply this information.

While at a children's party, a mom was talking about updating her resume. She has one child. I knew her husband had children from a previous marriage. I suggested she add them to her resume.

"Why would I do that?" she asked.

"Because the company will see that you only have one child. They will consider your age and come to the conclusion that you will most likely have more children. They may not hire you since they know you are allowed by law to take up to three years off from work," I said.

"You are absolutely right," she replied.

"And it's not lying. You consider and treat your husband's other children as your own children. Right?"

"Yes, of course. And they are my daughter's brother and sister."

Just as soon as it seems women are marching ahead into the workforce with college degrees and confidence, we have to slam on the brakes if we wish to have a family. We fall back into the 1950's - Leave it to Beaver - traditional mom stereotypes, and history repeats itself. Of course, not as extreme but the underlying problems are still there.

There are more divorces and single parents than ever in the United States. As women have gained more power over their reproductive rights and realize marriage is not an equal exchange for their unpaid labor, women leave their marriages. But women, along with their children, are living paycheck-to-paycheck in poverty.

But why? Even in progressive countries, like Germany, why does this continue to occur? It seems, women are punished in the work place for having children in any country. It stems from having a patriarchal society with its power structure: husbands lead and wives are dependent on them in traditional nuclear families.

Tear down these social barriers and culturally conditioned ideals! I realize there is not an easy solution, but there has to be some sort of balance. With all things in life and nature, there must be a balance or else the system fails. And this type of system is unsustainable in economies and at home. "If the human race is to survive we must find ways to prevent women from being disadvantaged if they choose to have children," Betty Friedan. [37]

SOLUTIONS

In the United States, now is the time to be more politically engaged and fight for a better system. And it's slowly happening! San Francisco (naturally) is the first U.S. city to offer six weeks paid parental leave beginning in 2017. [38] And New York state passed the nation's *first* 12-week paid family leave policy starting in 2018. [39]

How can *YOU* do something? Scott Wiener is the supervisor who sponsored the San Francisco proposal and made a great point. "What ends up happening is the state and sometimes even the federal government follows our lead...I'm confident other cities and states will take notice." He also remarked, "We shouldn't be forcing new mothers and fathers to choose between spending precious bonding time with their children and putting food on the table." [40] Folks, it always starts on a local level. U.S. Americans, start pushing your city to adapt the same laws as San Francisco (6 weeks) or New York state (12 weeks) or more! I encourage you to join like-minded individuals and join the movement. Yes, there is a movement! It's called gender equality.

I am overjoyed. As I write this chapter, a domino effect seems to be happening just as Scott Wiener said! A few days later, the state of California put a law into place that workers will receive up to six weeks of family-leave with 55% of their wages by 2018. [41]

These actions are a forward step; however, these small measures are ways of stalling by politicians. The U.S. needs massive reforms across the country and needs to extend *fully paid* family leave to *all* employees, not just companies with 20 to 50 employees or more. It's time for the U.S. president to do something and cross state lines that all U.S. citizens have the same rights as their neighboring states. And more importantly, implement laws to support gender equality at work and at home.

A country that demonstrates equality is Iceland. Yes, for the mom who really wants to have it all, buy yourself a Snow Mantra Parka Canada Goose coat and move to Iceland. Didn't Iceland experience one of the worst financial crisis in history you say? Yes! But after 2009 elected lesbian prime minister made half the government's cabinet women, they turned the economy around and continued gender equality by requiring supervisory boards at public companies to have 30% women as of 2012. [42]

And how has this progress affected women? According to the World Economic Forum's Global Gender Gap Report, Iceland ranks as the most gender-equal country in the world since 2009 with Finland, Norway, Sweden and Rwanda respectively in 2016. Germany came in 13th place, France in 17th and the United States took the 45th spot just beating Australia at number 46. What's going on down under?!

Deborah Steinborn and Uwe Jean Heuser are the authors of *Anders Denken! Warum Die Ökonomie Weiblicher Wird* [Thinking Differently: Why the Economy is Becoming More Female]. They explain, "Strong women, from the IMF's Christine Lagarde to Saudi Arabia's Lubna Olayan, are the heroes of our book. The world needs more of them. And they, in turn, need the world's support." [43]

In addition, the founder of the Veerni Project and the Global Foundation for Humanity, Jacqueline de Chollet has a most profound, clear solution. She says, "Education is the only thing you can do that will change society. Everything else is just a band-aid."

As I am finishing this book, I have learned about a concrete solution in the work place. In the first part of this chapter, I wrote about Anne-Marie Slaughter expressing how important it is for parents to have flexibility at work. There is an alternative work schedule called job sharing. It's one full time job share by two people. It's a perfect concept to help gender equality and integration. It enhances work-life balance and empowers working families; especially mothers returning to work from maternity leave.

In addition, mentoring programs for women are also beneficial. It can increase knowledge transfer, diversity and give opportunities for on-the-job training.

A YOUNG WOMAN ON HER OWN

I have been working since I was fifteen years old. I have experienced and a great deal of inequality at work. When I finally had the time, in my early 30's, I joined Radical Women in Los Angeles www.radicalwomen.org, "immersed in the daily fight against racism, sexism, homophobia, and labor exploitation." Also, I joined 9to5 www.9to5.org. An organization that supports working families. I was drawn to them because one of their main campaigns is for paid sick days. This meant a lot to me because of the continuous disagreements with my management.

A couple of years earlier, at one of my jobs in California, I got into an argument with my boss regarding sick pay. I worked there for three years and was not allowed any paid sick days, and I had only acquired two weeks paid vacation. I wanted to quit my job out of principal, but I also knew that there were no other jobs guaranteeing these simple humane requests. By California law, my boss was correct. He did not have to give me any paid sick days. Paid sick days are only a benefit if the company offers them when hired. As of 2016, there are only three cities in California that mandate paid sick days: San Francisco, Santa Monica, and, soon to come, Los Angeles. [44]

I once asked in a job interview what their policy is for sick days. "We don't really have *any* policies," she mumbled looking towards the ground. This was in the state of California not some right-to-work state.

And health insurance? The ten years I lived in NYC, I think I had health insurance five of those years. In my entire professional career, the health insurance offered by my companies always had high deductibles, and co-pays always hindering me from a doctor visit. Obviously, I never died except for that one time I got food poisoning and became severely dehydrated. By the third day, I knew something was severely wrong so, I couraged-up and called an ex-boyfriend (doctor). He gave me an IV (intravenous rehydration) and saved my kidneys.

It is either all or nothing in the States unless you have a government job or in the military. Ironic since one receives the most type of socialist benefits compared to the U.S. private sector. Jobs with the most benefits, for example, vacation, paid sick days, maternal and parental leave, come from the strongest union representation, for example, teachers, nurses, police and fire departments. In the U.S., women in unions tend to make $11,000 more a year. [45] Also, opportunities to make overtime pay and have a retirement plan.

I tell my two brothers, one is retired from the U.S. military and the other is a nurse, they have good government socialist jobs. This drives them mad! And, as of 2016, military women can receive twelve weeks of maternity leave! [46]

One company I worked at in New York City had a different set of rules every year. Some years, I had to use my precious vacation days for national holidays like Thanksgiving or the Fourth of July - no big deal - just the two most single important days of the year in the flag waving United States of America. Land of the free! But not free from company dictators and bought politicians.

THE NEW FEMINIST

During my time at university, a guest lecturer Kavita Ramdas (senior advisor to the Ford Foundation's president), gave the talk *Gender Equality for a Better Global Future.* [47] There was a chance for Q & A. My tiny little note got passed through the enormous sea of students, and it made its way on stage to Kavita. I asked, "Why is the word *feminist* such a negative word?" She put it simply, "Because it is a 'F' word." The audience roared with laughter. She went on to explain that the media for the past few decades has captured what a feminist is supposed to look like. Every time the news portrays a feminist it is always some angry woman shouting at the top of her lungs.

NOW…let's welcome Beyoncé and Taylor Swift. Yippee! Two

enormous super-stars that embrace and proudly wear the badge of honor *feminist*. And amazing people like Emma Watson who helped launch the *He For She* campaign fighting for gender equality. Celebrities may not be politicians but let's be honest, they have comic book, cultural, super powers. Nina Simone got it right by proclaiming that all artists have a duty to be involved in politics. "We will shape and mold this country or it will not be molded and shaped at all anymore. How can you be an artist and not reflect the times?"

GENDER DISCRIMINATION IS REAL

If this chapter does not convince you or someone else that gender pay inequality does not exist in the U.S., please google 'Gender Pay Inequality - Joint Economic Committee - US Senate'.

It is a report issued by the United States Congress - Joint Economic Committee in April 2016 that proves absolute discrimination based on gender.

I DON'T KNOW HOW SHE DOES IT

Another reason I was able to write this book is because Alec is in *kita* (daycare). Praise to *kitas*! As my friend Whitney, exclaims, "It saves mamas lives!" Additionally, it's critical for children to learn to socialize with other children and adults. [48]

Our German *kita* was a twelve-minute walk from our first home in Hamburg. When we rode my bike with Alec in the child bike seat, we flew there in two minutes. Alec loved it. The route we took has tree-lined streets and small boutiques. Plenty of different things for Alec to see and point out. He got most his thrills from constructions sites. Anything to do with large scaled machinery and trucks with flashing lights.

Alec went to *kita* for five hours a day, Monday to Friday. I would drop him off at 9:00am, and he ate breakfast at not extra cost. The *kita* also provides a lunch with no additional cost. After a two-hour nap, I would pick him up at 2:00pm.

The first month was all about transitioning into the *kita*. The first week I stayed with Alec at the *kita* for one and a half hours per day. The second week for three hours per day, but I waited in another room. The caretakers wanted me there in case Alec needed his mama, but he didn't! The third and fourth week Alec was doing five hours by himself, and I just had to be in the neighborhood on call. They only had to call me back one time. It was on a Monday. Mondays are always tough.

He did a great job transitioning. For me, it was slightly harder. At first, I was pulling a Lionel Richie and "dancing on the ceiling." But then I started to miss my lil' guy. Absence does make the heart grow fonder. I love my son. But him being at *kita* makes me miss and love him so much more. And jealous - the first few times I picked up Alec, he smelled of his caregiver's perfume!

For the first few months, I sang a song to him on our walk to *kita*: "Kita, kita, kita…we are going there. Kita, kita, kita…all our friends are there." Nothing really special but something that he recognized where we were going. Also, while I got Alec dressed and ready for *kita*, I emphasized and would say, "It's time to go see your friends and teachers. Who are your friends? Who are your teachers?" He loved this. Around twenty-two months, he started to list his favorite buddies.

The facility is a child's Peter Pan-fantasy land. Plenty of toys, books and play activities to keep our little darlings busy. And within the the huge outdoor play area, there is a small garden for them to learn about growing fruits and vegetables. Was Michelle Obama here?

A FEW GLITCHES IN THE SYSTEM

However, getting into a German *kita* proved to be difficult for us. Like all families in Hamburg, we had a free five hour per day voucher. If both parents are working full time, then the child receives an eight hour per day voucher. Even though the daycares in Germany are subsidized by the government, they are still a business and want to make money. If a family needs more than five hours per day, this is how the daycares turn a larger profit of course. Therefore, daycares want children who need care all day.

When we set out to find a *kita*, we thought we were golden. Since Jens worked for Airbus, we even had a preferential spot; didn't help one bit. A friend of mine is a doctor and her husband as well. When they sought out a space at the best *kita* in the neighborhood, it was theirs immediately. They needed child care for ten hours a day.

We ended up on four different waiting lists. Not one called us back. By chance, a brand new *kita* opened up, and they were looking to fill their spaces quickly. Jens and I were skeptical, but we checked it out and fell in love with the premises. It had an enormous outdoor play area, and the *kita* had sunlight pouring in. Decision made; not that we really had a choice.

LIFE AS A FAMILY

When Alec started *kita*, I thought I had become a part-time mom. In my head, this meant being a mom half the time and being 'me' half the time. But a couple of months into *kita*, I began to crunch the numbers. One would think five hours at *kita* is a good chunk of time.

Alec wakes up at 6:30am and goes to bed at 7:30pm. His wake time during the day is thirteen hours. So, actually I am two thirds mom and one third of the time, I get to be me.

I think the biggest struggle is how men (or partners) don't realize how much our lives change. A friend of mine overheard at a party that someone asked a new mom and dad, "Has anything changed in your lives since having the baby?" At the exact same time, the husband answered, "Nothing," and the wife replied, "Everything."

I am thankful for our *kita*. No matter how much we love our children, it is wonderful to have a little alone time or 'me time'. There are days when nighttime comes too quickly and days when Jens asks me at 6:00pm, "Is it Alec's bedtime yet?" But despite how exhausting the day was before, every morning is like Christmas morning. It's like a child racing to the Christmas tree and opening their gifts. Our excitement and love of walking into Alec's room in the morning, and scooping him up into our arms is the best gift of all.

Appendix A

The Why

My husband attends a lot of leadership training workshops at Airbus. One workshop was about understanding the reasons behind an assigned task. The trainee explained that if someone doesn't know the reason or the *why* behind a certain task, it will be a more difficult and longer process to achieve the assignment. Also, the employee might feel disconnected from the project and will not be as motivated resulting in a lower performance.

To be internally motivated, one must first ask why they are trying to achieve a goal. Understanding and believing in the *why* is crucial. This is used to address parenting techniques - especially when family members and close friends question them. How will you answer your mother-in-law when she asks why you are parenting a certain way?

Why? *Why did I write this book?* Because I felt a personal approach was needed in order to understand the more challenging aspects of child rearing and knowing the *why* behind each new learning process. Stories and personal experience validate an idea or suggestion. People are looking for knowledge and direction. And I feel if there is a problem worth solving then it should be worth sharing. As my dear friend, Francesca, always says, "Sharing is caring." For me, this is the most important parenting tip.

~ Marlane

I must be sobering and honest. When I began writing this book, it was for a selfish reason. I wanted to prove to myself and my son that I could do something else other than being a mom. I am one of the many stay-at-home-moms that put an immense amount of pressure, guilt and judgement on ourselves.

I also knew that I was the perfect candidate for catching the disease *The Feminine Mystique* as Betty Friedan described as "the problem that has no name."

I searched long and hard for a part-time job but nothing materialized. Due to economic and cultural circumstances, my work career was over. I came to the conclusion that my words might be the only value and power I had left. I turned inward and devised a plan. Through my son, I found meaning, hope and inspiration pushing me to put pen to paper.

Jo Frost (*Supernanny*) advises parents to do what is not only best for their baby but also what is best for themselves. For example, often parents say/think *I would die for you*. She suggests the attitude of *I would live for you*. [1] This spoke to me. It can have such a profound meaning depending on your situation.

But my selfish reason quickly changed to a different reason for writing this book: being more aware, involved and mindful of my son's learning and growth; in addition, the achievement of writing this book. I have never experienced a more gratifying path. As the author Fritz Stern wrote, "The reward of writing is learning." I would like to add "…and sharing."

"For all the dinners are cooked; the plates and cups washed; the children sent to school and gone out into the world. Nothing remains of it all. All has vanished. No biography or history has a word to say about it. And the novels, without meaning to, inevitable lie."

~ Virginia Woolf, *A Room of One's Own*

Appendix B

Citations

Chapter 1: Parenting: Learning Another Language

1. **sleep deprivation** Ellison, Katherine. *The Mommy Brain: How Motherhood Makes Us Smarter*. New York: Basic, 2005. 21. Print.

2. **"...the problem with stereotypes...only story." & TED talk** Adichie, C. (2009, May). Adichie, C.: The danger of a single story [Video file]. Retrieved from https://www.ted.com/talks/ chimamanda_adichie_the_danger_of_a_single_story? language=en#t-1100464

3. **trans fats** Ellison, Katherine. *The Mommy Brain: How Motherhood Makes Us Smarter.* New York: Basic, 2005. 186. Print.

4. **learning to read in Germany** Weiss, Luisa. "20 Surprising Things about Parenting in Germany." *A Cup of Jo*. Ed. Joanna Goddard. A Cup of Jo, 06 June 2016. Web. 05 Sept. 2016.

5. **"foster balanced bilingualism"** Treffers-Daller, Jeanine, and Carmen Silva-Corvalán. *Language Dominance in Bilinguals: Issues of Measurement and Operationalization*. Cambridge: Cambridge UP, 2016. 43. Print.

6. **"Most researchers...speakers."** Koll-Stobbe, Amei, and Sebastian (. Knospe. *Language Contact around the Globe: Proceedings of the LCTG3 Conference*. Vol. 5. Frankfurt Am Main: Peter Lang, 2014. 194. Print.

7. **one and four** Hogg, Tracy, and Melinda Blau. *Secrets of the Baby*

Whisperer for Toddlers. New York: Ballantine, 2003. 162. Print.

8. **"Though there are no studies...without confusion."** Dippel, Lennis, MD. *Trilingual By Six*. San Antonio, Texas: Lennis Dippel, 2015. 49. Print.

9. **"McLaughlin...mother tongue."** Foster-Cohen, Susan H. *Language Acquisition*. Houndmills, Basingstoke, Hampshire: Palgrave Macmillan, 2009. 244. Print.

Chapter 2: Parenting and Sleep

1. **"Infants, pre-toddlers, and toddlers...habits."** Ezzo, Gary, and Robert Bucknam. *On Becoming Baby Wise: Giving Your Infant the Gift of Nighttime Sleep*. Louisiana, MO: Parent-Wise Solutions, 2006. 53-54. Print.

2. **do not take your vitamins and/or iron supplements** Lu, Michael C. *Get Ready to Get Pregnant: Your Complete Prepregnancy Guide to Making a Smart and Healthy Baby*. New York, NY: Harper, 2009. 72. Print.

3. **consecutive three days (or less)** Hogg, Tracy, and Melinda Blau. *Secrets of the Baby Whisperer: How to Calm, Connect, and Communicate with Your Baby*. New York: Ballantine, 2001. 253, 261. Print.

4. **About one-third of American babies sleep through the night** Warner, Penny. *Smart Start for Your Baby: Your Baby's Development Week by Week during the First Year and How You Can Help*. Minnetonka, MN: Meadowbrook, 2001. 31. Print.

5. **usually after two or three months** Druckerman, Pamela. *Bringing up Bébé: One American Mother Discovers the Wisdom of French Parenting*. New York: Penguin, 2012. 40. Print.

6. **a hormone called melatonin** Cave, Simone, and Caroline Fertleman, Dr. *Your Baby Week by Week:*. London: Vermilion, 2007. 123. Print.

7. **wait a moment** Gaylord, James, and Michelle Hagen. *Your Baby's First Year for Dummies*. Hoboken, NJ: Wiley, 2005. 91. Print.

8. **The Pause** Druckerman, Pamela. *Bringing up Bébé: One American Mother Discovers the Wisdom of French Parenting*. New York: Penguin, 2012. 42-52. Print.

9. **"Caffeine...breastfeeding"**. Gaylord, James, and Michelle Hagen. *Your Baby's First Year for Dummies*. Hoboken, NJ: Wiley, 2005. 31. Print.

10. **dairy and gas-inducing foods** Gaylord, James, and Michelle Hagen. *Your Baby's First Year for Dummies*. Hoboken, NJ: Wiley, 2005. 95. Print.

11. **put him down before he falls asleep** Ezzo, Gary, and Robert Bucknam. *On Becoming Baby Wise: Giving Your Infant the Gift of Nighttime Sleep*. Louisiana, MO: Parent-Wise Solutions, 2006. 59. Print.

12. **comfort suck** Cave, Simone, and Caroline Fertleman, Dr. *Your Baby Week by Week:*. London: Vermilion, 2007. 84. Print.

13. **seven to eight hours continuously** Ezzo, Gary, and Robert Bucknam. *On Becoming Baby Wise: Giving Your Infant the Gift of Nighttime Sleep*. Louisiana, MO: Parent-Wise Solutions, 2006. 132. Print.

14. *controlled-crying* Frost, Jo. *Jo Frost's Confident Baby Care: What You Need to Know for the First Year from the UK's Most Trusted Nanny*. London: Orion, 2007. 167-69. Print.

15. **Try not to pick up your baby** Gaylord, James, and Michelle

Hagen. *Your Baby's First Year for Dummies*. Hoboken, NJ: Wiley, 2005. 163. Print.

16. **hold the child for a moment** Ezzo, Gary, and Robert Bucknam. *On Becoming Baby Wise: Giving Your Infant the Gift of Nighttime Sleep*. Louisiana, MO: Parent-Wise Solutions, 2006. 148. Print.

17. **it can last thirty-five minutes** Ezzo, Gary, and Robert Bucknam. *On Becoming Baby Wise: Giving Your Infant the Gift of Nighttime Sleep*. Louisiana, MO: Parent-Wise Solutions, 2006. 132. Print.

18. **15 minutes** Gaylord, James, and Michelle Hagen. *Your Baby's First Year for Dummies*. Hoboken, NJ: Wiley, 2005. 162. Print.

19. **"French experts...crying it out."** Druckerman, Pamela. *Bringing up Bébé: One American Mother Discovers the Wisdom of French Parenting*. New York: Penguin, 2012. 51-52. Print.

20. **bedtime routine** Hogg, Tracy, and Melinda Blau. *Secrets of the Baby Whisperer: How to Calm, Connect, and Communicate with Your Baby*. New York: Ballantine, 2001. 174. Print.

21. **a blanket or any object** Frost, Jo. *Jo Frost's Confident Baby Care: What You Need to Know for the First Year from the UK's Most Trusted Nanny*. London: Orion, 2007. 56. Print.

22. **"Feed every 3 to 4 hours...a pacifier."** Blakes, Albert L., M.D., and Sharon Rae, M.D. *Care of Your Infant*. N.p.: n.p., n.d. Print. Given to patient in the year 1976

23. **physical and mental** Gaylord, James, and Michelle Hagen. *Your Baby's First Year for Dummies*. Hoboken, NJ: Wiley, 2005. 152. Print.

24. **at six months** Warner, Penny. *Smart Start for Your Baby: Your Baby's Development Week by Week during the First Year and How You Can Help*. Minnetonka, MN: Meadowbrook, 2001. 70. Print.

25. **to follow the routine** Warner, Penny. *Smart Start for Your Baby: Your Baby's Development Week by Week during the First Year and How You Can Help*. Minnetonka, MN: Meadowbrook, 2001. 15. Print.

26. **symptom of hypothyroidism** "Hypothyroidism (underactive Thyroid)." *Symptoms and Causes*. Mayo Clinic, 10 Nov. 2015. Web. 18 Mar. 2016.

27. **Overactive and underactive thyroids** Stone, Joanne. *Pregnancy For Dummies 2nd Edition*. N.p.: n.p., 2004. 317. Print.

28. **postpartum thyroid dysfunction** "Postpartum Thyroid Dysfunction and Depression in an Unselected Population — NEJM." *New England Journal of Medicine*. New England Journal of Medicine, 20 June 1991. Web. 18 Mar. 2016.

29. **"can lead to...functioning."** Stein, Amy. *Heal Pelvic Pain: A Proven Stretching, Strengthening, and Nutrition Program for Relieving Pain, Incontinence, IBS, and Other Symptoms without Surgery*. New York: McGraw-Hill, 2009. Foreword x. Print.

30. **"custom for every...treatment."** Stein, Amy. *Heal Pelvic Pain: A Proven Stretching, Strengthening, and Nutrition Program for Relieving Pain, Incontinence, IBS, and Other Symptoms without Surgery*. New York: McGraw-Hill, 2009. Foreword ix. Print.

31. **"The National Institutes...life."** Manchester, Veronica. "Let Who Put What Where? Finding a Cure for Pelvic Pain." *ELLE*. ELLE, 27 Aug. 2013. Web. 31 Mar. 2016.

32. **"range from bones...irritation."** Stein, Amy. *Heal Pelvic Pain: A Proven Stretching, Strengthening, and Nutrition Program for Relieving Pain, Incontinence, IBS, and Other Symptoms without Surgery*. New York: McGraw-Hill, 2009. 15-16. Print.

33. **mostly acceptable for women to breastfeed (countries listed)**

Woods, Mark. *Planet Parent*. N.p.: White Ladder, 2015. 113-14. Print.

34. **good behavior** Hogg, Tracy, and Melinda Blau. *Secrets of the Baby Whisperer for Toddlers*. New York: Ballantine, 2003. 58. Print.

35. **the capacity to know** Ezzo, Gary, and Robert Bucknam. *On Becoming Pre-toddlerwise: From Babyhood to Toddlerhood (parenting Your Twelve to Eighteen Month Old)*. Louisiana, MO: Parent-Wise Solutions, 2008. 162-63. Print.

36. **instruct your toddler** Ezzo, Gary, and Robert Bucknam. *On Becoming Toddler Wise: Parenting the First Childhood Eighteen to Thirty-six Months*. Mt. Pleasant, SC.: Parent-Wise Solutions, 2003. 95. Print.

Chapter 3: Parenting and Food

1. **nursing with work** Ellison, Katherine. *The Mommy Brain: How Motherhood Makes Us Smarter*. New York: Basic, 2005. 211. Print.

2. **vegetables; no rice cereals or grains** Druckerman, Pamela. *Bringing up Bébé: One American Mother Discovers the Wisdom of French Parenting*. New York: Penguin, 2012. 201. Print.

3. **French kids** Druckerman, Pamela. *Bringing up Bébé: One American Mother Discovers the Wisdom of French Parenting*. New York: Penguin, 2012. 209. Print.

4. **cereals** Warner, Penny. *Smart Start for Your Baby: Your Baby's Development Week by Week during the First Year and How You Can Help*. Minnetonka, MN: Meadowbrook, 2001. 70. Print.

5. **cereals** Gaylord, James, and Michelle Hagen. *Your Baby's First*

Year for Dummies. Hoboken, NJ: Wiley, 2005. 136. Print.

6. **expert recommends pears** Hogg, Tracy, and Melinda Blau. *Secrets of the Baby Whisperer: How to Calm, Connect, and Communicate with Your Baby*. New York: Ballantine, 2001. 129. Print.

7. **glycaemic index foods** Cave, Simone, and Caroline Fertleman, Dr. *Your Baby Week by Week:*. London: Vermilion, 2007. 242. Print.

8. **tooth decay** Cave, Simone, and Caroline Fertleman, Dr. *Your Baby Week by Week:*. London: Vermilion, 2007. 236. Print.

9. **"In 2012, more...or obese."** "Childhood Obesity Facts." *Centers for Disease Control and Prevention*. Centers for Disease Control and Prevention, 27 Aug. 2015. Web. 29 Mar. 2016.

10. **29.1 million and 8.1 million** "National Diabetes Month — November 2015." *MMWR. Morbidity and Mortality Weekly Report MMWR Morb. Mortal. Wkly. Rep.* 64.45 (2015): 1261. Centers for Disease Control and Prevention. Web. 29 Mar. 2016.

11. **35.5 billion dollars** United States of America. United States Department of Agriculture. National Agricultural Statistics Service. *Dairy Cattle and Milk Production*. Vol. ACH12-14. N.p.: n.p., October 2014. Web. 25 Apr. 2016.

12. **Coca-Cola & Fairlife** Groden, Claire. "How Coke Is Trying to Turn 'Premium' Milk Into a Billion-Dollar Brand." *Fortune How Coke Is Trying to Turn Premium Milk Into a BillionDollar Brand Comments*. Fortune, 16 Mar. 2016. Web. 22 Apr. 2016.

13. **"The dairy industry...you. It's a lie...tried."** MacBoock. "Apple Confidential - Steve Jobs on "Think Different" - Internal Meeting Sept. 23, 1997." *YouTube*. YouTube, 05 Nov. 2013. Web. 25 Apr. 2016.

14. **rBH hormone** Escobar, Christine. "The Tale of RBGH, Milk, Monsanto and the Organic Backlash." *The Huffington Post.* TheHuffingtonPost.com, 2 Apr. 2009. Web. 25 Apr. 2016.

15. **"about one million…ears"** "Myringotomy (Ear Tubes) in Children." *Myringotomy (Ear Tubes) | Boston Children's Hospital.* Boston Children's Hospital, n.d. Web. 26 Apr. 2016.

16. **"the most common…old"** "Myringotomy (Ear Tubes) in Children." *Myringotomy (Ear Tubes) | Boston Children's Hospital.* Boston Children's Hospital, n.d. Web. 26 Apr. 2016.

Chapter 4: Parenting and the Potty

1. **"the right kind…to learn."** Hogg, Tracy, and Melinda Blau. *Secrets of the Baby Whisperer for Toddlers.* New York: Ballantine, 2003. 134. Print.

2. **between eighteen months and two years** Hogg, Tracy, and Melinda Blau. *Secrets of the Baby Whisperer for Toddlers.* New York: Ballantine, 2003. 133-34. Print.

3. **"estimated 50%…one"** Woods, Mark. *Planet Parent: The World's Best Ways to Bring Up Your Children.* Richmond, UK: Vacation Works Pubs (UK), 2015. 101. Print.

4. **week's worth of diapers** McMahon, Tom, and Remo Cerruti. *Kid Tips: Proven Child-care Tips from Experienced Parents across the Country.* New York, NY: Pocket, 1998. 51. Print.

5. **six thousand disposable diapers** Spurrier, Juliet, MD, and Alison Buck. "Cloth Diapers vs. Disposables: How and What to Choose?" *BabyGearLab.com.* BabyGearLab, 09 July 2015. Web. 11 Sept. 2016.

6. **risk of urinary and bowel problems** Woods, Mark. *Planet Parent:*

The World's Best Ways to Bring Up Your Children. Richmond, UK: Vacation Works Pubs (UK), 2015. 99. Print.

7. **potato chips, candy, soda, cake and salted nuts** Ezzo, Gary, and Robert Bucknam. *On Becoming Toddler Wise: Parenting the First Childhood Eighteen to Thirty-six Months*. Mt. Pleasant, SC.: Parent-Wise Solutions, 2003. 117-18. Print.

8. **nighttime dryness** Green, Christopher, and Roger Roberts. *New Toddler Taming: A Parents' Guide to the First Four Years*. London: Vermilion, 2006. 242. Print.

9. **Facebook post and comments** Nigbur (Wingo), Marlane. "Night time bed wetting blues." Facebook. 4 Aug. 2015. Web. 9 Sept. 2016.

Chapter 5: Parenting and the Other

1. **other person's humanity** Druckerman, Pamela. *Bringing up Bébé: One American Mother Discovers the Wisdom of French Parenting*. New York: Penguin, 2012. 155. Print.

2. **piano lessons at three** Chua, Amy. *Battle Hymn of the Tiger Mother*. New York: Penguin, 2011. 9. Print.

3. **Suzuki piano books/method** Chua, Amy. *Battle Hymn of the Tiger Mother*. New York: Penguin, 2011. 26-27. Print.

4. **"My mother…sell them."** Ellison, Katherine. *The Mommy Brain: How Motherhood Makes Us Smarter*. New York: Basic, 2005. 189. Print.

5. **time critical before six years** Dippel, Lennis, MD. *Trilingual By Six*. San Antonio, Texas: Lennis Dippel, 2015. 84. Print.

6. **"through play, social interaction and participation."** Dippel,

Lennis, MD. *Trilingual By Six*. San Antonio, Texas: Lennis Dippel, 2015. 142. Print.

7. **NAEYC encourages this play-based** Dippel, Lennis, MD. *Trilingual By Six*. San Antonio, Texas: Lennis Dippel, 2015. 23. Print.

8. **language acquisition device** Dippel, Lennis, MD. *Trilingual By Six*. San Antonio, Texas: Lennis Dippel, 2015. 3. Print.

9. **"designed not…word."** Dippel, Lennis, MD. *Trilingual By Six*. San Antonio, Texas: Lennis Dippel, 2015. 48. Print.

10. **functional neuroimaging** Dippel, Lennis, MD. *Trilingual By Six*. San Antonio, Texas: Lennis Dippel, 2015. 50. Print.

11. **"the natural wealth…ect."** "natural resources". Dictionary.com Unabridged. Random House, Inc. 04 Apr. 2016. <Dictionary.com http://www.dictionary.com/browse/natural-resources>.

12. **stereotypes, judgement or a power struggle & TED talk** Selasi, T. (2014, October). Taiye Selasi: Don't ask where I'm from, ask where I'm a local [Video file]. Retrieved from https://www.ted.com/talks/taiye_selasi_don_t_ask_where_i_m_from_ask_where_i_m_a_local

13. **six months or seven months** "Buying a Playpen." *BabyCentre*. BabyCentre, Feb. 2014. Web. Mar. 2016.

14. **fresh and alert** Ezzo, Gary, and Robert Bucknam. *On Becoming Baby Wise: Giving Your Infant the Gift of Nighttime Sleep*. Louisiana, MO: Parent-Wise Solutions, 2006. 211. Print.

15. **independent play** Bucknam, Nanny. "Playpens: Are They Good or Bad?" *NannySavvy*. NannySavvy, 13 June 2013. Web. 16 Mar. 2016.

16. **stay put in playpen** Ezzo, Gary, and Robert Bucknam. *On*

Becoming Pre-toddlerwise: From Babyhood to Toddlerhood (parenting Your Twelve to Eighteen Month Old). Louisiana, MO: Parent-Wise Solutions, 2008. 155. Print.

17. **overuse does mean neglect** Frost, Jo. *Jo Frost's Confident Baby Care: What You Need to Know for the First Year from the UK's Most Trusted Nanny*. London: Orion, 2007. 52. Print.

18. **follow-up tip** McMahon, Tom, and Remo Cerruti. *Kid Tips: Proven Child-care Tips from Experienced Parents across the Country*. New York, NY: Pocket, 1998. 146-47. Print.

19. **before a tantrum** Nicholls, Lucy. *Toddlers: The Mumsnet Guide*. London: Bloomsbury, 2009. 17. Print.

20. **decision making** Nicholls, Lucy. *Toddlers: The Mumsnet Guide*. London: Bloomsbury, 2009. 15. Print.

21. **clear communication** Green, Christopher, and Roger Roberts. *New Toddler Taming: A Parents' Guide to the First Four Years*. London: Vermilion, 2006. 74. Print.

22. **adult teeth** Nicholls, Lucy. *Toddlers: The Mumsnet Guide*. London: Bloomsbury, 2009. 29. Print.

23. **beyond the age of two** Frost, Jo. *Jo Frost's Confident Baby Care: What You Need to Know for the First Year from the UK's Most Trusted Nanny*. London: Orion, 2007. 190-91. Print.

Bonus Chapter 6: Passports

1. **"individual acts...difference."** Stern, Fritz Richard. *Five Germanys I Have Known*. New York: Farrar, Straus and Giroux, 2006. 10. Print.

Bonus Chapter 7: Cross-border Collaboration

1. **"Child care…a year nationwide."** Hill, Catey. "The 10 Most Expensive Places to Raise a Family in the U.S." *MarketWatch*. MarketWatch, 19 Mar. 2016. Web. 09 May 2016.

2. **"Only a high school…necessary…"** Paquette, Danielle. "The $90 Billion Question: Do We Need Government-supplied Daycare?" *The Washington Post*. The Washington Post, 6 Apr. 2016. Web. 8 Apr. 2016.

3. **two year program** Eddy, Melissa. "German Child Care Workers' Strike Brings Debate on Priorities." *The New York Times*. The New York Times, 05 June 2015. Web. 08 Apr. 2016.

4. **to be licensed or** United States of America. National Association of Child Care Resource & Referral Agencies. *Leaving Children to Chance*. N.p.: n.p., March 2012. Print.

5. **"In the long run…system."** Paquette, Danielle. "The $90 Billion Question: Do We Need Government-supplied Daycare?" *The Washington Post*. The Washington Post, 6 Apr. 2016. Web. 8 Apr. 2016.

6. **average of $10.31 per hour** Paquette, Danielle. "The $90 Billion Question: Do We Need Government-supplied Daycare?" *The Washington Post*. The Washington Post, 6 Apr. 2016. Web. 8 Apr. 201

7. **"Caring for children…us?"** Slaughter, Anne-Marie. "The Failure of the Phrase 'Work-Life Balance'" *The Atlantic*. Atlantic Media Company, 16 Dec. 2015. Web. 19 Apr. 2016.

8. **high-quality, affordable childcare, pre-kindergarten programs, and after-school activities** Ellison, Katherine. *The Mommy Brain: How Motherhood Makes Us Smarter*. New York: Basic, 2005. 210. Print.

9. **"Perhaps the biggest...missing."** Bassett, Laura. "The U.N. Sent 3 Foreign Women To The U.S. To Assess Gender Equality. They Were Horrified." *Huffpost Politics*. The Huffington Post, 16 Dec. 2015. Web. 19 Apr. 2016.

10. **"a vague undefined wish...the children."** Friedan, Betty. *The Feminine Mystique*. London: Penguin, 2010. 44. Print.

11. **People can feel empty with housework** Friedan, Betty. *The Feminine Mystique*. London: Penguin, 2010. 196. Print.

12. **"the need for self-fulfillment"** Friedan, Betty. *The Feminine Mystique*. London: Penguin, 2010. 263. Print.

13. **Anne-Marie Slaughter regarding "having it all"** Slaughter, Anne-Marie. "Why Women Still Can't Have It All." *The Atlantic*. Atlantic Media Company, July-Aug. 2012. Web. 20 Apr. 2016.

14. **U.S. Department of Labor** Andrews, Edmund L. "Survey Confirms It: Women Outjuggle Men." *The New York Times*. N.p., 15 Sept. 2004. Web. 22 Mar. 2016.

15. **"Ensuring equality on the home front"** Lam, Bourree. "How Do We Close the Wage Gap in the U.S.?" *The Atlantic*. Atlantic Media Company, 8 Mar. 2016. Web. 28 June 2016.

16. **50 employees or less** "Wage and Hour Division (WHD)." *Family and Medical Leave Act*. United States Department of Labor, n.d. Web. 23 Mar. 2016.

17. **50 employees or less** "ECFR — Code of Federal Regulations." *ECFR — Code of Federal Regulations*. United States Government Publishing Office, n.d. Web. 23 Mar. 2016.

18. **"The UK guarantees...leave."** Wills, Amanda. "New York Just Passed the Nation's Most Radical Paid Family Leave Policy."

Mashable. Mashable, 2 Apr. 2016. Web. 04 Apr. 2016.

19. **"We need to rethink...looks like."** Valente, Joanna. "Sheryl Sandberg Admits She Got It Wrong with 'Lean In'" *Kveller*. Kveller, 09 May 2016. Web. 10 May 2016.

20. **The Fair Labor Standards Act of 1938** Grossman, Jonathan. "U.S. Department of Labor -- History -- Fair Labor Standards Act of 1938:." *U.S. Department of Labor -- History -- Fair Labor Standards Act of 1938:*. U.S. Department of Labor, n.d. Web. 05 Apr. 2016.

21. **"When racism...inequality worsens."** Danks, Lois. "Closing the Gender Pay Gap: What Will It Take?" *Freedom Socialist Voice of Revolutionary Feminism*. Freedom Socialist Party, June 2015. Web. 28 June 2016.

22. **Pope Francis, "Why...less than men? The disparity... scandal."** Ohlheiser, Abby, and Michelle Boor Stein. "Pope Francis: It's 'pure Scandal' That Women Earn Less than Men for the Same Work." *Washington Post*. The Washington Post, 29 Apr. 2015. Web. 28 June 2016.

23. **Mommy Gap** Ellison, Katherine. *The Mommy Brain: How Motherhood Makes Us Smarter*. New York: Basic, 2005. 163. Print.

24. **denied jobs or less pay** McNally, Terrence. "The Mommy Wage Gap." *Alternet*. Alternet, 11 June 2006. Web. 23 Mar. 2016.

25. **"Men seldom suffer...stability."** Ellison, Katherine. *The Mommy Brain: How Motherhood Makes Us Smarter*. New York: Basic, 2005. 163. Print.

26. **men receive higher pay** Gilles, Kate, and Charlotte Feldman-Jacobs. *Preventing Gender-biased Sex Selection: An Interagency Statement OHCHR, UNFPA, UNICEF, UN Women and WHO*. Geneva: World Health Organization (WHO), 2011. *When Technology and Tradition Collide: From Gender Bias to Sex Selection*. Population

Reference Bureau, Sept. 2012. Web. 5 Apr. 2016.

27. **retirement packages** "Female Infanticide." *Ethics Guide*. BBC, 2014. Web. 5 Apr. 2016.

28. **the World Bank reported** World Bank, *World Development Report 2012: Gender Equality and Development* (Washington, DC: World Bank, 2011).

29. **Gender pay gap** "Women in Germany Await Workplace Equality." *DW.COM*. Deutsche Welle, 08 Mar. 2016. Web. 14 Nov. 2016.

30. **Members of the DAX** Bennhold, Katrin. "Women Nudged Out of German Workforce." *The New York Times*. The New York Times, 28 June 2011. Web. 14 Nov. 2016.

31. **"But at…isn't working."** "Merkel Party Leader Admits Sexism Is a Problem." *The Local*. The Local.de, 25 Sept. 2016. Web. 14 Nov. 2016.

32. **The G7 is "among the worst…with 15%."** Medland, Dina. "Today's Gender Reality In Statistics, Or Making Leadership Attractive To Women." *Forbes*. Forbes Magazine, 7 Mar. 2016. Web. 14 Nov. 2016.

33. **"one of Chancellor Angela Merkel's pet projects"** Mkenya Ujerumani. "German High Court Declares Betreuungsgeld Unconstitutional." *Mkenya Ujerumani*. Mkenya Ujerumani, 03 Aug. 2015. Web. 15 Sept. 2016.

34. **"until 1977, …to work."** Rayasam, Renuka. "Why Germany's New Quota for Women On Boards Looks Like a Bust." *Fortune*. Fortune, 10 Mar. 2016. Web. 14 Nov. 2016.

35. **Extending school hours and offering after school activities** Daley, Suzanne, and Nicholas Kulish. "Germany Fights Population

Drop." *The New York Times*. The New York Times, 13 Aug. 2013.
Web. 19 Apr. 2016.

36. **negative growth rate** Rosenberg, Matt. "Why Is Negative
Population Growth Important?" *About.com Education*. About.com, 22
July 2016. Web. 15 Sept. 2016.

37. **"If the human race…children."** Center for American Women
and Politics. "Conversation with Betty Friedan (Talking Leadership
Series)." *YouTube*. Rutgers The State University of New Jersey, 19
Dec. 2014. Web. 29 June 2016.

38. **San Francisco** Levin, Sam. "San Francisco Becomes First U.S.
City to Mandate Fully Paid Parental Leave." *theguardian*. N.p., 5 Apr.
2016. Web. 6 Apr. 2016.

39. **12-week paid family leave policy** Wills, Amanda. "New York
Just Passed the Nation's Most Radical Paid Family Leave Policy."
Mashable. Mashable, 2 Apr. 2016. Web. 04 Apr. 2016.

40. **"What ends up…notice." & "We shouldn't…table."** Levin,
Sam. "San Francisco Becomes First U.S. City to Mandate Fully Paid
Parental Leave." *theguardian*. N.p., 5 Apr. 2016. Web. 6 Apr. 2016.

41. **In the state of California** McGreevy, Patrick. "Brown Signs
California Law Boosting Paid Family-leave Benefits." *Los Angeles
Times*. Los Angeles Times, 11 Apr. 2016. Web. 13 Apr. 2016.

42. **But after 2009 elected** Steinborn, Deborah, and Uwe Jean
Heuser. "Gender Über Alles." *World Policy Journal* Spring
XXXI.N*1 (2014): n. pag. Web. 5 Nov. 2016.

43. **"Strong women, from…support."** Heuser, Uwe Jean, and
Deborah Steinborn. "Women Hold the Key to the Economy of the
Future." *World Economic Forum*. World Economic Forum, 30 Oct.

2013. Web. 5 Nov. 2016.

44. **mandate paid sick days** Reyes, Emily Alpert. "6 Paid Sick Days for Workers in L.A.? City Council Says Yes." *Los Angeles Times*. Los Angeles Times, 19 Apr. 2016. Web. 20 Apr. 2016.

45. **In the U.S., women in unions...a year.** Danks, Lois. "Closing the Gender Pay Gap: What Will It Take?" *Freedom Socialist Voice of Revolutionary Feminism*. Freedom Socialist Party, June 2015. Web. 28 June 2016.

46. **Navy and Marine Corps** Ferdinando, Lisa. "Carter Announces 12 Weeks Paid Military Maternity Leave, Other Benefit." U.S. Department of Defense, 28 Jan. 2016. Web. 05 Apr. 2016.

47. **Ramadas, Kavita**. "Gender Equality for a Better Global Future." California State University, Dominguez Hills. 29 Sept. 2011. Lecture.

48. **socialization** Green, Christopher, and Roger Roberts. *New Toddler Taming: A Parents' Guide to the First Four Years*. London: Vermilion, 2006. 299. Print.

Appendix A - Why

1. **advises parents** Frost, Jo. *Jo Frost's Confident Baby Care: What You Need to Know for the First Year from the UK's Most Trusted Nanny*. London: Orion, 2007. 72. Print.

Recipes

I didn't allow Alec to have any sugar before the age of two. I became obsessed making baked goods with bananas and applesauce - such a great sugar substitute.

Bon appétit ~
Guten Appetit ~
Enjoy your meal ~

Sugar Free Banana Bread

Ingredients:
- 4 large or 5 medium ripe bananas (1 ½ cups)*
- ½ cup no sugar added applesauce
- 1 egg
- 1/4 cup vegetable oil
- 1 tablespoon vanilla extract
- 1 ½ cups flour
- 1 teaspoon baking soda
- 1 teaspoon cinnamon

Directions:
1. Preheat oven to 340 F (170 C) degrees.
2. Blend/mash bananas
3. With a hand mixer, beat egg, oil, applesauce and vanilla. Then add bananas and mix until creamy.
4. In a separate bowl, mix flour, baking soda and cinnamon.
5. Gradually add dry mixture to wet ingredients.

Pour batter into a lightly oiled 9-by-5-inch or 8x4 loaf pan. Or non-stick muffin tin. Makes 24 muffins. Do not use paper baking cups because the cake will stick to the paper. If you don't have a non-stick pan, butter/oil the pan or muffin tin.

Bake for 40 minutes if using a loaf pan (15-18 minutes for muffins) or insert a toothpick until it comes out clean. Before slicing bread, cool on wire rack.

This recipe is great to double. The bread and/or muffins freeze well.

* If you don't have enough bananas, add applesauce to make up for the rest.

Banana Bread (sugar added)

Ingredients:
- 4 large or 5 medium ripe bananas (1 ½ cups)*
- 1 egg
- 3/4 cup sugar
- 1/2 cup vegetable oil
- 1 tablespoon vanilla extract
- 1 ½ cups flour
- 1 teaspoon baking soda
- 1 teaspoon cinnamon
- 1/2 cup chopped nuts (optional)
- 1 chocolate bar (optional)

Directions:
1. Preheat oven to 340 F (170 C) degrees.
2. Blend/mash bananas
3. With a hand mixer, beat egg, oil and vanilla. Then add bananas and mix until creamy.
4. In a separate bowl, mix flour, baking soda and cinnamon.
5. Gradually add dry mixture to wet ingredients.

Pour batter into a lightly oiled and floured 9-by-5-inch or 8x4 loaf pan . Or non-stick muffin tin. Makes 24 muffins. Do not use paper baking cups because the cake will stick to the paper. If you don't have a non-stick pan, butter/oil the pan or muffin tin.

Bake for 40 minutes if using a loaf pan (15-18 minutes for muffins) or insert a toothpick until it comes out clean. Before slicing, cool on wire rack.

This recipe is great to double. The bread and muffins freeze well.

* If you don't have enough bananas, add applesauce to make up for the rest.

Sugar Free Banana Pancakes

Ingredients:
- 1 ripe banana
- 2 eggs
- 1 teaspoon vanilla extract
- ½ cups flour

Directions:
1. Blend bananas, eggs and vanilla.
2. Gradually add flour.
3. Pour into hot buttered pan - cook on medium heat.

Makes 6 small/medium pancakes. Serves 2 adults and 1 toddler.

Enjoy them plain or top with applesauce, jam, syrup, honey or nut spread.

Banana Pumpkin Bread (sweetened with honey)

Ingredients:
- 2 large ripe bananas
- 2 eggs
- 1 1/3 cup pumpkin purée (11 ounces) *
- ½ cup honey
- 1/3 vegetable oil
- 2 ½ cups flour
- 3 teaspoons cinnamon
- 1 teaspoon baking soda
- 1 teaspoon baking powder

Directions:
1. Preheat oven to 350 F (180 C) degrees.
2. Blend/mash bananas
3. Beat eggs
4. With a hand mixer, beat eggs, pumpkin, bananas, honey and oil until creamy.
5. In a separate bowl, mix flour, cinnamon, baking soda and baking powered.
6. Gradually add dry mixture to wet ingredients.

Pour batter into a gently oiled 9-by-5-inch loaf pan and spread evenly. Or a muffin tin. Do not use paper baking cups because the cake will stick to the paper.

Bake for 45 minutes (15-20 minutes for muffins) or insert a toothpick until it comes out clean. Before slicing bread, cool on wire rack.

* If you don't have enough pumpkin, add bananas or applesauce to make up for the rest.

Oatmeal Cookies (low sugar)

Ingredients·
- 1 cup quick oats
- 1 cup flour
- 1/2 cup no sugar added applesauce
- 1/2 melted butter or vegetable oil
- 1 egg
- 1/4 cup sugar
- 2 tablespoons honey
- 1 tablespoon baking powder
- 1/3 cup unsalted sunflower seeds*

Directions:
1. Preheat oven to 340 F (170 C) degrees.
2. With a hand mixer, beat butter, egg, and sugar together. Then beat in applesauce and honey.
4. In a separate bowl, mix oats, flour, baking powder and soda.
5. Gradually add dry mixture to wet ingredients. Then sunflower seeds.

Use 2 cookie baking sheets. Makes 24 cookies.

Bake for 10 minutes. Cool on wire rack.

The cookies freeze well.

*Optional or any other nuts

About the Author

Marlane is a self-proclaimed writer. She has a fancy degree but not from a fancy school. Her passion for learning comes from all genres, but her favorite is geography. She wishes to spark your curiosity and lend a helping hand with raising your little ones. Her family resides in Hamburg, Germany, but the next layover will most likely be in Toulouse, France.

www.marlanewingo.com
PINTEREST: marlanewingo
TWITTER: @WingoMarlane
INSTAGRAM: marlanewingo
FACEBOOK: Marlane Wingo

17918992R00135

Printed in Poland
by Amazon Fulfillment
Poland Sp. z o.o., Wrocław